A Midsummer Night's Dream

A Midsummer Night's Dream

As Directed by
John Hirsch

Edited by
Elliott Hayes
and
Michal Schonberg

Costume Sketches by
Desmond Heeley

CBC Enterprises/Les Entreprises Radio-Canada
MONTRÉAL • TORONTO • NEW YORK • LONDON

Published by CBC Enterprises/Les Entreprises Radio-Canada, a division of the Canadian Broadcasting Corporation, Box 500, Station A, Toronto (Ontario), Canada M5W 1E6, in association with The Stratford Shakespearean Festival Foundation of Canada, Box 520, Stratford (Ontario), Canada N5A 6V2.

Publié par CBC Enterprises/Les Entreprises Radio-Canada, une division de la Société Radio-Canada, C.P. 500, Succursale «A», Toronto (Ontario), Canada M5W 1E6, en collaboration avec la Stratford Shakespearean Festival Foundation of Canada, C.P. 520, Stratford (Ontario), Canada N5A 6V2.

The Artistic Director of The Stratford Shakespearean Festival is John Hirsch.

CANADIAN CATALOGUING IN PUBLICATION DATA

Shakespeare, William, 1564-1616.
  A midsummer night's dream
Stratford Festival ed.
ISBN 0-88794-136-2

I. CBC Enterprises. II. Title.
PR2827.A1 1984   822.3'3   C84-098521-5

Publisher/Éditeur: Glenn Edward Witmer
Editor/Révision: Betty Corson
Design/Conception graphique: Leslie Smart and Associates Limited
Layout and Assembly/Magnettes et mise en pages: First Image
Typesetter/Composition: CompuScreen Typesetting Limited
Printer/Impression: D. W. Friesen and Sons Limited

Printed and bound in Canada

1 2 3 4 5 6 7 / 90 89 88 87 86 85 84

Contents

Observations on
A Midsummer Night's Dream
By John Hirsch

A *Midsummer Night's Dream* is a fairy tale – direct, rich in texture, humorous, and full of adventure. Fairy tales are not only entertaining; they also deal with primitive and deep-seated feelings, urges, and ideas. As Bruno Bettelheim has shown in his book *The Uses of Enchantment*, they reveal how human beings think and feel.

Shakespeare's *Dream* embodies the Renaissance idea that the universe is organically comprehensive and comprehensible. Although many people no longer espouse such a belief, they still have a tremendous need for an image of moral order and completeness that gives them some understanding about their place in the scheme of things. And that's why people are so greatly affected by Shakespeare's comedies and romances. In *A Midsummer Night's Dream*, one of his most miraculous early plays, every single part reflects every other part. I think it's essential for people to be presented with such an image of wholeness. Personally, I wouldn't know how to exist without it.

When I do one of Shakespeare's works, I'm not only investigating the play, I'm also exploring who and where I am at that particular moment. A production comes alive when the people who are working on it undergo a process of self-examination through their total commitment to the play.

I have found that all of Shakespeare's comedies and romances present a conflict between the male and female principles, and the *Dream* explores this conflict more thoroughly than any other play. It opens with the subjugation of the Amazons by Theseus and his army; Hippolyta, the queen of the Amazons, is being forced to marry Theseus, whose society is totally male-chauvinistic. The conflict between Hippolyta and Theseus is played out fully through Titania and Oberon, their immortal alter egos.

Society becomes unhealthy and the universe topsy-turvy when there is no balanced union between the male and female principles, the yin and yang. Because of the quarrel between Titania and Oberon, the earth and the cosmos are in disarray. Titania says to Oberon:

> ... The spring, the summer,
> The childing autumn, angry winter, change

1

Their wonted liveries; and the mazéd world,
By their increase, now knows not which is which.
And this same progeny of evils comes
From our debate, from our dissension:
We are their parents and original.

(Act II/Scene 1, lines 111-17)

The play moves from disorder to even greater disorder, and then toward recuperation and health. Finally, in the last act, we have a ritualistic celebration of love triumphant in the marriage of Hippolyta and Theseus. Life-enhancing harmony has been restored to the universe mainly because the argument between Titania and Oberon, or the female and male principles, has been resolved.

It is also important to note that the moon presides over the play. *A Midsummer Night's Dream* is about the power of the moon – about luna, lunacy, and the goddess of the moon, Diana, who is a huntress. The moon has a powerful effect on human beings; it changes our perceptions and emotions, the way we see and feel. In the moonlit forest the *Dream's* characters go through horrendous experiences: they literally go mad under the light of the moon. But having been immersed in lunacy, they reach sanity and a perception and understanding of cosmic wholeness and their place within it.

The difference between illusion and reality is a central concern in *A Midsummer Night's Dream*. As Helena says, the most vital perception is *through*, not with, the eye; the mind, or imagination, is the human power that gives things form and meaning. The people in the *Dream* have their perception changed by forces both within and beyond themselves. Puck tells Oberon about the lunatic behaviour of the "mechanicals" in the forest:

Their sense thus weak, lost with their fears thus strong,
Made senseless things begin to do them wrong.

(Act III/Scene 2, lines 27-28)

And near the end of the play Theseus sums up the transforming power of love and the imagination in his famous speech about the lunatic, the lover, and the poet (Act V/*Scene 1*, in particular lines 4-17).

I've learned a lot about *A Midsummer Night's Dream* by reading Bruno Bettelheim, Carl Jung, R. D. Laing, and Jan Kott, who was the first to explore the play's dark side. "The Dream is the most erotic of Shakespeare's plays," Kott wrote. "In no other tragedy or comedy of his, except *Troilus and Cressida*, is the eroticism expressed so brutally."

Drawing upon various sources as well as my own intuitions and reflections, I arrive at a point of view for any given play. Victor Hugo said something that illuminates for me the *Dream* as a metaphor for the illusion and reality of the theatre:

"The theatre is not the land of the real: there are cardboard trees, canvas palaces, a sky of rags, glass diamonds, brassy gold, gilt on the lily, rouge on the cheek and a sun that comes out from under the earth.

"The theatre is the land of the real: there are human hearts on the stage, human hearts backstage, human hearts in the audience."

The choreographer George Ballanchine once said that his aim was "to make audiences see music and hear dancing." That tidbit suggests a great deal about the importance of music and dance in the *Dream*. For Shakespeare, music and sleep are restorative powers, and dance is his ritualistic celebration of the union of men and women.

But of all the aspects of this or any play, the most important element of all, of course, is the language. For only when a word is *experienced* – in three dimensions, as it were – do we know what a word is. A word must be tasted, swallowed, and digested to become flesh. Actors, especially, have to learn to taste language. The energy of Shakespeare's plays is in his use of language – the incredible rush of articulation that comes from some tremendous need in his characters to express themselves through words.

It's fascinating to go through Shakespeare's plays and find words that occur and recur. *A Midsummer Night's Dream* is rich in "moon," "eye," and "amazed." The characters are amazed over and over again because what comes to pass is so wondrous for everyone. Indeed, the *Dream* itself amazes.

John S. Hirsch

Patricia Conolly as Titania

A Note to
the Reader

The text used in the Stratford Festival Edition of *A Midsummer Night's Dream* is based upon the Globe Text, with reference to the First Folio. It incorporates generally accepted modern spellings and punctuations.

A glossary of Elizabethan and unfamiliar terms appears at the bottom of the pages.

The Act and Scene numbers are given at the top of each right-hand page. The Scene numbers enclosed in brackets in the right-hand margin indicate the way in which the play was divided for rehearsal purposes at Stratford. During a performance the stage manager would use these Scene numbers to call light, orchestra, and sound cues.

Also in the right-hand margin is the over-all numerical delineation; the Stratford Festival Edition delineation is enclosed in brackets. The SFE line numbers refer the reader to a set of emendations at the end of the text. These emendations include word changes, line changes, cuts, and additions that were made specifically for the 1984 Stratford Festival Production of *A Midsummer Night's Dream*.

The 1984 Stratford Festival Production of

A Midsummer Night's Dream

Directed by John Hirsch
Designed by Desmond Heeley
Lighting designed by Michael J. Whitfield
Fight staging by B. H. Barry
Choreography by Kelly Robinson

The Cast (in order of appearance)

Theseus, Duke of Athens	Nicholas Pennell
Hippolyta, Queen of the Amazons	Patricia Conolly
Philostrate, Master of the Revels	Jack Medley
Egeus, Hermia's father	Max Helpmann
Hermia	Mary Haney
Demetrius, Hermia's suitor	Benedict Campbell
Lysander, loved by Hermia	Joseph Ziegler
Helena	Rosemary Dunsmore
Peter Quince, a carpenter	William Needles
Francis Flute, a bellows-mender	Simon Bradbury
Tom Snout, a tinker	Kenneth Pogue
Robin Starveling, a tailor	Edward Atienza
Snug, a joiner	Les Carlson
Nick Bottom, a weaver	Brian Bedford
Puck	Diego Matamoros
Oberon, King of the Fairies	Nicholas Pennell
Titania, Queen of the Fairies	Patricia Conolly

Peaseblossom		Toni LoRaso
Cobweb	Titania Fairies	Danny Kohn
Moth		Ron Rees
Mustardseed		Ernest Harrop

Oberon Fairies	Christopher Gibson
	Bill Johnston
	Shane Kelly
	Greg Lawson

Other Fairies	Brent Stait
	Janet Macdonald
	Jan Wood

Drummer   Tim Whelan

Gardeners, Amazons, Soldiers, Courtiers:
Caro Coltman, Holly Dennison, Daniel Dion, David Elliott,
Christopher Gibson, Charles Kerr, Danny Kohn, Greg Lawson,
Elizabeth Leigh-Milne, Toni LoRaso, Janet Macdonald, Jefferson Mappin,
Kevin McNulty, Tracey Olson, Ron Rees, Michael Shepherd,
Tim Whelan, Jan Wood

Alternates:

Bottom	Shaun Austin-Olsen
Starveling	Keith Dinicol
Theseus/Oberon	Stephen Russell

Assistant Director:	Brian Rintoul
Stage Manager:	Michael Shamata
Assistant Stage Managers:	Lesley MacMillan and Jill Orenstein
Assistant Designer:	Polly Scranton Bohdanetzky
Assistant Lighting Designers:	Elizabeth Asselstine and Louise Guinand

TRESSELLS.
NICHOLAS PE

HEESEY '84

A MIDSUMMER NIGHTS DREAM.   STRATFORD ONTAR

Act First

Scene 1

The hall in the palace of Duke Theseus

Theseus and Hippolyta enter and take their seats,
followed by Philostrate and attendants

Theseus	Now, fair Hippolyta, our nuptial hour	[1]

Theseus   Now, fair Hippolyta, our nuptial hour
Draws on apace: four happy days bring in
Another moon: but O, methinks how slow
This old moon wanes! She lingers my desires,
Like to a step-dame, or a dowager,
Long withering out a young man's revenue.

Hippolyta   Four days will quickly steep themselves in night:
Four nights will quickly dream away the time:
And then the moon, like a silver bow
New-bent in heaven, shall behold the night   10
Of our solemnities.

Theseus   Go, Philostrate,
Stir up the Athenian youth to merriments,
Awake the pert and nimble spirit of mirth,
Turn melancholy forth to funerals:
The pale companion is not for our pomp.
                    Philostrate bows and departs
Hippolyta, I wooed thee with my sword,
And won thy love doing thee injuries;
But I will wed thee in another key:
With pomp, with triumph, and with revelling.

Enter Egeus and his daughter Hermia,
followed by Lysander and Demetrius

[1] All numbers in brackets refer to Emendations, pp. 101–107. See also Note,
p. 5.

Egeus	*(bows)* Happy be Theseus, our renowned duke.	20
Theseus	Thanks, good Egeus. What's the news with thee?	
Egeus	Full of vexation come I, with complaint	

Egeus *(bows)* Happy be Theseus, our renowned duke. 20
Theseus Thanks, good Egeus. What's the news with thee?
Egeus Full of vexation come I, with complaint
Against my child, my daughter Hermia.
Stand forth, Demetrius. My noble lord,
This man hath my consent to marry her.
Stand forth, Lysander. And, my gracious duke,
This man hath witched the bosom of my child.
Thou, thou, Lysander, thou hast given her rhymes,
And interchanged love-tokens with my child:
Thou hast by moonlight at her window sung, 30
With feigning voice, verses of feigning love:
And stol'n the impression of her fantasy
With bracelets of thy hair, rings, gauds, conceits,
Knacks, trifles, nosegays, sweetmeats – messengers
Of strong prevailment in unhardened youth.
With cunning hast thou filched my daughter's heart,
Turned her obedience, which is due to me,
To stubborn harshness. And, my gracious duke,
Be it so she will not here before your grace
Consent to marry with Demetrius, 40
I beg the ancient privilege of Athens.
As she is mine, I may dispose of her;
Which shall be either to this gentleman,
Or to her death; according to our law
Immediately provided in that case.
Theseus What say you, Hermia. Be advised, fair maid:
To you your father should be as a god;
One that composed your beauties; yea and one
To whom you are but as a form in wax
By him imprinted, and within his power 50
To leave the figure or disfigure it.
Demetrius is a worthy gentleman.
Hermia So is Lysander.
Theseus   In himself he is:
But in this kind, wanting your father's voice,
The other must be held the worthier.
Hermia I would my father looked but with my eyes.
Theseus Rather your eyes must with his judgement look.
Hermia I do entreat your grace to pardon me.
I know not by what power I am made bold;

---

33 **gauds:** toys
   conceits: trinkets
34 **Knacks:** knickknacks
35 **prevailment:** influence

Max Helpmann as Egeus, to Hermia, played by Mary Haney:
  "Full of vexation come I, with complaint
  Against my child, my daughter Hermia."

	Nor how it may concern my modesty	60
	In such a presence here to plead my thoughts:	
	But I beseech your grace that I may know	
	The worst that may befall me in this case	
	If I refuse to wed Demetrius.	
Theseus	Either to die-the death, or to abjure	
	For ever the society of men.	
	Therefore, fair Hermia, question your desires,	
	Know of your youth, examine well your blood,	
	Whether, if you yield not to your father's choice,	
	You can endure the livery of a nun,	70
	For aye to be a shady cloister mewed,	
	To live a barren sister all your life,	
	Chanting faint hymns to the cold fruitless moon.	
	Thrice blesséd they that master so their blood,	
	To undergo such maiden pilgrimage:	
	But earthlier happy is the rose distilled,	
	Than that which withering on the virgin thorn	
	Grows, lives and dies in single blessedness.	
Hermia	So will I grow, so live, so die, my lord,	
	Ere I will yield my virgin patent up	80
	Unto his lordship, whose unwishéd yoke	
	My soul consents not to give sovereignty.	
Theseus	Take time to pause, and by the next new moon –	
	The sealing-day betwixt my love and me	
	For everlasting bond of fellowship –	
	Upon that day either prepare to die	
	For disobedience to your father's will,	
	Or else to wed Demetrius as he would,	
	Or on Diana's altar to protest	
	For aye austerity and single life.	90
Demetrius	Relent, sweet Hermia – and, Lysander, yield	
	Thy crazéd title to my certain right.	
Lysander	You have her father's love, Demetrius;	
	Let me have Hermia's: do you marry him.	
Egeus	Scornful Lysander! True, he hath my love;	
	And what is mine my love shall render him.	
	And she is mine, and all my right of her	
	I do estate unto Demetrius.	
Lysander	I am, my lord, as well derived as he,	
	As well possessed: my love is more than his:	100

---

71 **aye:** ever
   mewed: confined
73 **moon:** as in Diana, goddess of chastity
99 **derived:** descended

	My fortunes every way as fairly ranked –	
	If not with vantage – as Demetrius':	
	And, which is more than all these boasts can be,	
	I am beloved of beauteous Hermia.	
	Why should not I then prosecute my right?	
	Demetrius, I'll avouch it to his head,	
	Made love to Nedar's daughter, Helena,	
	And won her soul; and she, sweet lady, dotes,	
	Devoutly dotes, dotes in idolatry,	
	Upon this spotted and inconstant man.	110
Theseus	I must confess that I have heard so much:	
	And with Demetrius thought to have spoke thereof;	
	But, being over-full of self-affairs,	
	My mind did lose it. But Demetrius come,	
	And come Egeus, you shall go with me:	
	I have some private schooling for you both.	
	For you, fair Hermia, look you arm yourself	
	To fit your fancies to your father's will;	
	Or else the law of Athens yields you up –	
	Which by no means we may extenuate –	120
	To death, or to a vow of single life.	
	Come, my Hippolyta: what cheer, my love?	
	Demetrius and Egeus, go along:	
	I must employ you in some business	
	Against our nuptial, and confer with you	
	Of something nearly that concerns yourselves.	
Egeus	With duty and desire we follow you.	

All depart save Hermia and Lysander [Scene 2]

Lysander	How now, my love? Why is your cheek so pale?	
	How chance the roses there do fade so fast?	
Hermia	Belike for want of rain, which I could well	130
	Beteem them from the tempest of my eyes.	
Lysander	Ay me! For aught I could ever read,	
	Could ever hear by tale or history,	
	The course of true love never did run smooth;	
	But, either it was different in blood.	
Hermia	O cross! Too high to be enthralled to low.	
Lysander	Or else misgraffèd in respect of years.	
Hermia	O spite! Too old to be engaged to young.	
Lysander	Or else it stood upon the choice of friends.	
Hermia	O hell! To choose love by another's eyes!	140

---

106 **to his head:** to his face
110 **spotted:** stained
135 **blood:** rank, birth
137 **misgraffèd:** mismatched

13

Lysander	Or, if there were a sympathy in choice,
	War, death, or sickness did lay siege to it –
	Making it momentany as a sound, [143]
	Swift as a shadow, short as any dream,
	Brief as the lightning in the collied night,
	That, in a spleen, unfolds both heaven and earth;
	And ere a man hath power to say 'Behold!'
	The jaws of darkness do devour it up:
	So quick bright things come to confusion.
Hermia	If then true lovers have been ever crossed, 150
	It stands as an edict in destiny:
	Then let us teach our trial patience,
	Because it is a customary cross,
	As due to love as thoughts and dreams and sighs,
	Wishes and tears; poor Fancy's followers.
Lysander	A good persuasion: therefore hear me, Hermia:
	I have a widow aunt, a dowager
	Of great revénue, and she hath no child:
	From Athens is her house remote seven leagues:
	And she respects me as her only son. 160
	There, gentle Hermia, may I marry thee:
	And to that place the sharp Athenian law
	Cannot pursue us. If thou lovest me then,
	Steal forth thy father's house to-morrow night;
	And in the wood, a league without the town,
	Where I did meet thee once with Helena,
	To do observance to a morn of May,
	There will I stay for thee.
Hermia	My good Lysander,
	I swear to thee by Cupid's strongest bow,
	By his best arrow with the golden head, 170
	By the simplicity of Venus' doves,
	By that which knitteth souls and prospers loves,
	And by that fire which burned the Carthage queen, [173-74]
	When the false Troyan under sail was seen,
	By all the vows that ever men have broke –
	In number more than ever women spoke –
	In that same place thou hast appointed me,
	To-morrow truly will I meet with thee.
Lysander	Keep promise, love. Look, here comes Helena.

---

145 **collied:** blackened
146 **spleen:** fit of passion
155 **Fancy:** love
156 **persuasion:** principle
171 **Venus' doves:** sacred doves drew Venus's chariot

Benedict Campbell as Demetrius, Patricia Conolly as Hippolyta,
and Nicholas Pennell as Theseus. Theseus:
  "I must employ you in some business
  Against our nuptial, and confer with you . . ."

Lysander, played by Joseph Ziegler, to Hermia:
 "If thou lovest me then,
  Steal forth thy father's house tomorrow night."

Enter Helena [Scene 3]

Hermia	God speed, fair Helena: whither away? 180
Helena	Call you me fair? That 'fair' again unsay.
	Demetrius loves your fair: O happy fair!
	Your eyes are lode-stars, and your tongue's sweet air
	More tuneable than lark to shepherd's ear,
	When wheat is green, when hawthorn buds appear.
	Sickness is catching: O, were favour so,
	Yours would I catch, fair Hermia, ere I go –
	My ear should catch your voice, my eye your eye,
	My tongue should catch your tongue's sweet melody.
	Were the world mine, Demetrius being bated, 190
	The rest I'd give to be to you translated.
	O, teach me how you look, and with what art
	You sway the motion of Demetrius' heart.
Hermia	I frown upon him; yet he loves me still.
Helena	O that your frowns would teach my smiles such skill.
Hermia	I give him curses; yet he gives me love.
Helena	O that my prayers could such affection move.
Hermia	The more I hate, the more he follows me.
Helena	The more I love, the more he hateth me.
Hermia	His folly, Helena, is no fault of mine. 200
Helena	None, but your beauty; would that fault were mine.
Hermia	Take comfort: he no more shall see my face:
	Lysander and myself will fly this place.
	Before the time I did Lysander see,
	Seemed Athens as a paradise to me:
	O then, what graces in my love do dwell,
	That he hath turned a heaven unto a hell!
Lysander	Helen, to you our minds we will unfold:
	To-morrow night, when Phoebe doth behold
	Her silver visage in the wat'ry glass, 210
	Decking with liquid pearl the bladed grass –
	A time that lovers' flights doth still conceal –
	Through Athens' gates have we devised to steal.
Hermia	And in the wood, where often you and I
	Upon faint primrose-beds were wont to lie,
	Emptying our bosoms of their counsel sweet,
	There my Lysander and myself shall meet,
	And thence from Athens turn away our eyes,

---

183 **lode-stars:** guiding stars
184 **tuneable:** musical
190 **bated:** excepted
209 **Phoebe:** the moon
215 **wont:** accustomed

17

	To seek new friends and stranger companies.	
	Farewell, sweet playfellow: pray thou for us;	220
	And good luck grant thee thy Demetrius!	
	Keep word, Lysander: we must starve our sight	
	From lovers' food till tomorrow deep midnight.	*Exit*
Lysander	I will, my Hermia. Helena, adieu:	
	As you on him, Demetrius dote on you!	*Exit*
Helena	How happy some o'er other some can be!	
	Through Athens I am thought as fair as she,	
	But what of that? Demetrius thinks not so:	
	He will not know what all but he do know.	
	And as he errs, doting on Hermia's eyes,	230
	So I, admiring of his qualities.	
	Things base and vile, holding no quantity,	
	Love can transpose to form and dignity.	
	Love looks not with the eyes, but with the mind:	
	And therefore is winged Cupid painted blind.	
	Nor hath Love's mind of any judgement taste:	
	Wings and no eyes figure unheedy haste.	
	And therefore is Love said to be a child:	
	Because choice he is so oft beguiled.	
	As waggish boys in game themselves forswear:	240
	So the boy Love is perjured every where.	
	For ere Demetrius looked on Hermia's eyne,	
	He hailed down oaths that he was only mine.	
	And when this hail some heat from Hermia felt,	
	So he dissolved, and showers of oaths did melt.	
	I will go tell him of fair Hermia's flight:	
	Then to the wood will he to-morrow night	
	Pursue her: and for this intelligence	
	If I have thanks, it is a dear expense:	
	But herein mean I to enrich my pain,	250
	To have his sight thither and back again.	*Exit*

Scene 2

[Scene 4]

Quince, Bottom, Snug, Flute, Snout and Starveling

Quince	Is all our company here?
Bottom	You were best to call them generally, man by man, according to the scrip.

---

240 **waggish:** playful

Rosemary Dunsmore as Helena:
  "Love looks not with the eyes, but with the mind:
  And therefore is winged Cupid painted blind."

Quince	Here is the scroll of every man's name,
	which is thought fit, through all Athens, to play
	in our interlude before the duke and
	the duchess, on his wedding-day at night.
Bottom	First, good Peter Quince, say what
	the play treats on; then read the names
	of the actors; and so grow to a point.
Quince	Marry, our play is, The most lamentable comedy
	and most cruel death of Pyramus and Thisbe.
Bottom	A very good piece of work, I assure you,
	and a merry. Now, good Peter Quince, call forth your
	actors by the scroll. Masters, spread yourselves.
Quince	Answer, as I call you. Nick Bottom, the weaver.
Bottom	Ready: name what part I am for, and proceed.
Quince	You, Nick Bottom, are set down for Pyramus.
Bottom	What is Pyramus? A lover, or a tyrant?
Quince	A lover that kills himself, most gallant, for love.
Bottom	That will ask some tears in the true performing of it.
	If I do it, let the audience look to their eyes:
	I will move storms: I will condole in some measure.
	To the rest – yet my chief humour is for a tyrant.
	I could play Ercles rarely, or a part to tear a cat in,
	to make all split.

10
[11]

20

> The raging rocks
> And shivering shocks
> Shall break the locks
>   Of prison-gates,
> And Phibbus' car
> Shall shine from far
> And make and mar
>   The foolish Fates.

30

	This was lofty. Now name the rest of the players.
	This is Ercles' vein, a tyrant's vein; a lover is
	more condoling.
Quince	Francis Flute, the bellows-mender.
Flute	Here, Peter Quince.
Quince	Flute, you must take Thisbe on you.
Flute	What is Thisbe? A wandring knight?
Quince	It is the lady that Pyramus must love.
Flute	Nay, faith: let me not play a woman:
	I have a beard coming.
Quince	That's all one: you shall play it in a mask:

40

---

6 **interlude:** play
23 **condole:** show grief
24 **humour:** inclination
25 **Ercles:** Hercules

	and you may speak as small as you will.
Bottom	An I may hide my face, let me play Thisbe too.
	I'll speak in a monstrous little voice. Thisne, thisne – 'Ah,
	Pyramus, my lover dear, thy Thisbe dear, and lady dear.'
Quince	No, no, you must play Pyramus; 50
	and Flute, you Thisbe.
Bottom	Well, proceed.
Quince	Robin Starveling, the tailor.
Starveling	Here, Peter Quince.
Quince	Robin Starveling, you must play Thisbe's mother.
	Tom Snout, the thinker.
Snout	Here, Peter Quince.
Quince	You, Pyramus' father; myself, Thisbe's father;
	Snug, the joiner, you the lion's part: and I hope
	here is a play fitted. 60
Snug	Have you the lion's part written? Pray you,
	if it be, give it me: for I am slow of study.
Quince	You may do it extempore: for it is nothing
	but roaring.
Bottom	Let me play the lion too. I will roar, that I will
	do any man's heart good to hear me. I will roar,
	that I will make the duke say, 'Let him roar again:
	let him roar again.'
Quince	An you should do it too terribly, you would fright
	the duchess and the ladies, that they would shriek: 70
	and that were enough to hang us all.
All	That would hang us, every mother's son.
Bottom	I grant you, friends, if that you should fright the
	ladies out of their wits, they would have no more
	discretion but to hang us: but I will aggravate my voice
	so, that I will roar you as gently as any sucking dove:
	I will roar you an 'twere any nightingale.
Quince	You can play no part but Pyramus: for Pyramus is a
	sweet-faced man; a proper man as one shall see in a
	summer's day; a most lovely, gentleman-like man: 80
	therefore you must needs play Pyramus.
Bottom	Well. I will undertake it. What
	beard were I best to play it in?
Quince	Why, what you will.
Bottom	I will discharge it in either your straw-colour
	beard, your orange-tawny beard, your
	purple-in-grain beard, or your French-crown-colour

---

75 **aggravate:** mistake for "moderate"
86 **orange-tawny:** dark yellow
  purple-in-grain: fast-dyed with red tint
87 **French-crown:** gold coin

Kenneth Pogue as Snout, William Needles as Quince, Edward Atienza as
Starveling, Les Carlson as Snug, Brian Bedford as Bottom.
Bottom: "I will roar you an 'twere any nightingale."
Quince: "You can play no part but Pyramus: for Pyramus is a sweet-faced
  man . . ."

	beard, your perfect yellow.
Quince	Some of your French crowns have no hair at all;
	and then you will play barefaced. *(He distributes* [90]
	strips of paper among them.) But, masters, here are your
	parts, and I am to entreat you, request you, and desire
	you, to con them by to-morrow night; and meet me in
	the palace wood, a mile without the town, by moon-
	light; there will we rehearse; for if we meet in the city,
	we shall be dogged with company, and our devices
	known. In the meantime, I will draw a bill of proper-
	ties, such as our play wants. I pray you, fail me not.
Bottom	We will meet, and there we may rehearse most obscenely,
	and courageously. Take pains, be perfect: adieu. 100
Quince	At the duke's oak we meet.
Bottom	Enough: hold, or cut bow-strings. *Exeunt*

---

89 **French crowns:** refers to baldness caused by venereal disease
99 **obscenely:** possible mistake for "seemly" (correctly)
100 **be perfect:** know your lines

A MIDSUMMER NIGHT'S DREAM.   TITANIA'S TRAIN

HEELEY '84

TO LOOK LIKE RAGAMUFFINS —
SUNBURNT. — V. SOFT + WORN
FABRICS. OLD CORSETS — GOSSAMER
SPONGES. SNAIL TRAILS.
MOTHS — THE HAIR SHOULD BE
AS THIN AS POSS. LIKE AN OLD
DANDELION CLOCKS — TINY PIECES OF
GLASS — DROPS! — TARNISHED SILVER

SHOULD LOOK LIKE
'REAL CLOTHES' MOILED
OVER, — SHOULD HAVE
BASKETS + PARCELS?

Act Second

Scene 1
[Scene 5]

The palace wood, a league from Athens

Puck and a Fairy, meeting

Puck	How now, spirit! Whither wander you?
Fairy	Over hill, over dale,
	Thorough bush, thorough briar,
	Over park, over pale,
	Thorough flood, thorough fire.
	I do wander every where.
	Swifter than the moonës sphere: [7]
	And I serve the Fairy Queen,
	To dew her orbs upon the green.
	The cowslips tall her pensioners be, 10
	In their gold coats spots you see:
	Those be rubies, fairy favours:
	In those freckles live their savours.
	I must go seek some dewdrops here,
	And hang a pearl in every cowslip's ear.
	Farewell, thou lob of spirits: I'll be gone –
	Our queen and all her elves come here anon.
Puck	The king doth keep his revels here to-night.
	Take heed the queen come not within his sight.
	For Oberon is passing fell and wrath, 20
	Because that she as her attendant hath
	A lovely boy, stol'n from an Indian king:
	She never had so sweet a changeling. [23]
	And jealous Oberon would have the child

---

4 **pale:** fenced land
16 **lob:** clown
20 **passing fell:** exceedingly angry

	Knight of his train, to trace the forests wild.	
	But she, perforce, witholds the lovéd boy,	
	Crowns him with flowers, and makes him all her joy.	
	And now they never meet in grove, or green,	
	By fountain clear, or spangled starlight sheen,	
	But they do square – that all their elves, for fear,	30
	Creep into acorn-cups and hide them there.	
Fairy	Either I mistake your shape and making quite,	
	Or else you are that shrewd and knavish sprite	
	Called Robin Goodfellow. Are not you he	
	That frights the maidens of the villagery,	
	Skim milk, and sometimes labour in the quern,	
	And bootless make the breathless housewife churn,	
	And sometime make the drink to bear no barm,	
	Mislead night-wanderers, laughing at their harm?	
	Those that Hobgoblin call you and sweet Puck,	40
	You do their work, and they shall have good luck.	
	Are not you he?	
Puck	Thou speak'st aright;	
	I am that merry wanderer of the night.	
	I jest to Oberon, and make him smile	
	When I a fat and bean-fed horse beguile,	
	Neighing in likeness of a filly foal;	
	And sometime lurk I in a gossip's bowl,	
	In very likeness of a roasted crab,	
	And, when she drinks, against her lips I bob,	
	And on her withered dewlap pour the ale.	50
	The wisest aunt, telling the saddest tale,	
	Sometime for three-foot stool mistaketh me:	
	Then slip I from her bum, down topples she,	
	And 'tailor' cries, and falls into a cough:	[54]
	And then the whole quire hold their hips and loff,	
	And waxen in their mirth, and neeze, and swear	
	A merrier hour was never wasted there.	
	But room, faëry: here comes Oberon.	
Fairy	And here my mistress. Would that he were gone.	

The clearing is suddenly thronged with fairies: [Scene 6]
Oberon and Titania confront each other

---

30 **square:** quarrel
36 **quern:** handmill for grinding corn
37 **bootless:** fruitless
38 **barm:** froth on ale
45 **beguile:** trick
47 **gossip:** old woman
48 **crab:** crabapple, used in a drink
50 **dewlap:** loose skin on the neck
55 **quire;** company
loff: laugh
56 **waxen:** increase
neeze: sneeze

Oberon	Ill met by moonlight, proud Titania.	60
Titania	What, jealous Oberon! Fairies, skip hence –	
	I have forsworn his bed and company.	
Oberon	Tarry, rash wanton. Am not I thy lord?	
Titania	Then I must be thy lady: but I know	
	When thou hast stol'n away from fairy land,	
	And in the shape of Corin sat all day,	
	Playing on pipes of corn, and versing love,	
	To amorous Phillida. Why art thou here,	
	Come from the farthest steep of India?	
	But that, forsooth, the bouncing Amazon,	70
	Your buskined mistress and your warrior love,	
	To Theseus must be wedded; and you come	
	To give their bed joy and prosperity.	
Oberon	How canst thou thus for shame, Titania,	
	Glance at my credit with Hippolyta,	
	Knowing I know thy love to Theseus?	
	Didst thou not lead him through the glimmering night	
	From Perigouna, whom he ravishéd?	
	And make him with fair Ægles break his faith,	
	With Ariadne, and Antiopa?	80
Titania	These are the forgeries of jealousy:	[81-117]
	And never, since the middle summer's spring,	
	Met we on hill, in dale, forest, or mead,	
	By pavéd fountain, or by rushy brook,	
	Or in the beachéd margent of the sea,	
	To dance our ringlets to the whistling wind,	
	But with thy brawls thou hast disturbed our sport.	
	Therefore the winds, piping to us in vain,	
	As in revenge, have sucked up from the sea	
	Contagious fogs: which falling in the land,	90
	Hath every pelting river made so proud,	
	That they have overborne their continents.	
	The ox hath therefore stretched his yoke in vain,	
	The ploughman lost his sweat, and the green corn	
	Hath rotted ere his youth attained a beard:	
	The fold stands empty in the drownéd field,	
	And crows are fatted with the murrion flock,	
	The nine men's morris is filled up with mud,	

97 **murrion:** murrain (a disease of sheep and cattle)

Cobweb, played by Danny Kohn, in background, Oberon,
played by Nicholas Pennell:
  "Ill met by moonlight, proud Titania,"
Titania: "What, jealous Oberon! Fairies, skip hence –
  I have forsworn his bed and company."

And the quaint mazes in the wanton green
For lack of tread are undistinguishable.   100
The human mortals want their winter cheer.   [101]
No night is now with hymn or carol blest.
Therefore the moon, the governess of floods,
Pale in her anger, washes all the air,
That rheumatic diseases do abound:
And thorough this distemperature we see
The seasons alter: hoary-headed frosts
Fall in the fresh lap of the crimson rose,
And on old Hiems' thin and icy crown
An odorous chaplet of sweet summer buds   110
Is, as in mockery, set. The spring, the summer,
The childing autumn, angry winter, change
Their wonted liveries; and the mazéd world,
By their increase, now knows not which is which.
And this same progeny of evils comes
From our debate, from our dissension:
We are their parents and original.

Oberon   Do you amend it then: it lies in you.
Why should Titania cross her Oberon?
I do but beg a little changeling boy,   120
To be my henchman.

Titania   Set your heart at rest,
The fairy land buys not the child of me.
His mother was a vot'ress of my order:
And in the spicéd Indian air, by night,
Full often hath she gossiped by my side,
And sat with me on Neptune's yellow sands,
Marking th' embarkéd traders on the flood;
When we have laughed to see the sails conceive
And grow big-bellied with the wanton wind:
Which she, with pretty and with swimming gait   130
Following – her womb then rich with my young squire –
Would imitate, and sail upon the land,
To fetch me trifles, and return again,
As from a voyage, rich with merchandise.
But she, being mortal, of that boy did die;
And for her sake do I rear up her boy,
And for her sake I will not part with him.

---

109 **Hiem:** winter
112 **childing:** bountiful
113 **wonted:** accustomed
     liveries: distinctive suit
123 **vot'ress:** votaress, devoted worshipper
127 **traders:** trading ships

Oberon	How long within this wood intend you stay?
Titania	Perchance, till after Theseus' wedding-day.
	If you will patiently dance in our round, 140
	And see our moonlight revels, go with us:
	If not, shun me, and I will spare your haunts.
Oberon	Give me that boy, and I will go with thee.
Titania	Not for thy fairy kingdom. – Fairies, away!
	We shall chide downright, if I longer stay.

Titania departs in anger with her train   [Scene 7]

Oberon	Well: go thy way. Thou shalt not from this grove,
	Till I torment thee for this injury.
	My gentle Puck, come hither. Thou remembrest
	Since once I sat upon a promontory,
	And heard a mermaid on a dolphin's back 150
	Uttering such dulcet and harmonious breath,
	That the rude sea grew civil at her song,
	And certain stars shot madly from their spheres,
	To hear the sea-maid's music.
Puck	I remember.
Oberon	That very time I saw – but thou couldst not –
	Flying between the cold moon and the earth,
	Cupid all armed: a certain aim he took
	At a fair Vestal, thronéd by the west, [158]
	And loosed his love-shaft smartly from his bow,
	As it should pierce a hundred thousand hearts: 160
	But I might see young Cupid's fiery shaft
	Quenched in the chaste beams of the wat'ry moon:
	And the imperial Vot'ress passéd on,
	In maiden meditation, fancy-free.
	Yet marked I where the bolt of Cupid fell.
	It fell upon a little western flower;
	Before, milk-white; now purple with love's wound –
	And maidens call it, Love-in-idleness.
	Fetch me that flower; the herb I showed thee once.
	The juice of it, on sleeping eyelids laid, 170
	Will make or man or woman madly dote
	Upon the next live creature that it sees.
	Fetch me this herb, and be thou here again
	Ere the leviathan can swim a league.
Puck	I'll put a girdle around about the earth
	In forty minutes. *Exit*

---

171 **dote**: foolishly in love
174 **leviathan**: sea monster (whale)

Oberon to Puck, played by Diego Matamoros:
  "Fetch me this herb, and be thou here again
  Ere the leviathan can swim a league."
Puck: "I'll put a girdle around the earth
  In forty minutes."

Oberon	Having once this juice,

Oberon   Having once this juice,
I'll watch Titania when she is asleep:
And drop the liquor of it in her eyes:
The next thing then she waking looks upon –
Be it on lion, bear, or wolf, or bull,   180
On meddling monkey, or on busy ape –
She shall pursue it with the soul of love,
And ere I take this charm from off her sight –
As I can take it with another herb –
I'll make her render up her page to me.
But who comes here? I am invisible,
And I will overhear their conference.

Demetrius enters the clearing, Helena following him   [Scene 8]

Demetrius   I love thee not; therefore pursue me not.
Where is Lysander and fair Hermia?
The one I'll slay; the other slayeth me.   190
Thou told'st me they were stol'n unto this wood:
And here am I, and wood within this wood,
Because I cannot meet my Hermia.
Hence, get thee gone, and follow me no more.

Helena   You draw me, you hard-hearted adamant;
But yet you draw not iron, for my heart
Is true as steel. Leave you your power to draw,
And I shall have no power to follow you.

Demetrius   Do I entice you? Do I speak you fair
Or rather do I not in plainest truth   200
Tell you I do not nor I cannot love you?

Helena   And even for that do I love you the more:
I am your spaniel; and, Demetrius,
The more you beat me, I will fawn on you.
Use me but as your spaniel: spurn me, strike me,
Neglect me, lose me: only give me leave,
Unworthy as I am, to follow you.
What worser place can I beg in your love –
And yet a place of high respect with me –
Than to be uséd as you use your dog?   210

Demetrius   Tempt not too much the hatred of my spirit,
For I am sick when I do look on thee.

Helena   And I am sick when I look not on you.

---

192 **and wood:** and mad
195 **adamant:** magnet
199 **speak you fair:** say nice things

Demetrius to Helena: "Tempt not too much the hatred of my spirit,
  For I am sick when I do not look on thee."
Helena: "And I am sick when I look not on you."

Demetrius	You do impeach your modesty too much,	
	To leave the city and commit yourself	
	Into the hands of one that loves you not,	
	To trust the opportunity of night	
	And the ill counsel of a desert place	
	With the rich worth of your virginity.	
Helena	Your virtue is my privilege: for that	220
	It is not night when I do see your face,	
	Therefore I think I am not in the night –	
	Nor doth this wood lack worlds of company,	
	For you in my respect are all the world.	
	Then how can it be said I am alone,	
	When all the world is here to look on me?	
Demetrius	I'll run from thee and hide me in the brakes,	
	And leave thee to the mercy of wild beasts.	
Helena	The wildest hath not such a heart as you.	
	Run when you will: the story shall be changed;	230
	Apollo flies, and Daphne holds the chase;	[231]
	The dove pursues the griffin; the mild hind	
	Makes speed to catch the tiger – bootless speed,	
	When cowardice pursues and valour flies.	
Demetrius	I will not stay thy questions – let me go:	
	Or, if thou follow me, do not believe	
	But I shall do thee mischief in the wood.	*Exit*
Helena	Ay, in the temple, in the town, the field,	
	You do me mischief. Fie, Demetrius!	
	Your wrongs do set a scandal on my sex:	240
	We cannot fight for love, as men may do;	
	We should be wooed and were not made to woo.	
	I'll follow thee and make a heaven of hell,	
	To die upon the hand I love so well.	*Exit*
Oberon	Fare thee well, nymph. Ere he do leave this grove,	
	Thou shalt fly him, and he shall seek thy love.	

Puck reappears   [Scene 9]

	Hast thou the flower there? Welcome, wanderer.	
Puck	Aye, there it is.	
Oberon	I pray thee, give it me.	
	I know a bank where the wild thyme blows,	
	Where oxlips and the nodding violet grows,	250
	Quite over-canopied with luscious woodbine,	
	With sweet musk-roses, and with eglantine:	

214 **impeach:** discredit
modesty: reputation
233 **bootless:** useless

34

There sleeps Titania, some time of the night,
Lulled in these flowers with dances and delight:
And there the snake throws her enamelled skin,
Weed wide enough to wrap a fairy in.
And with the juice of this I'll streak her eyes,
And make her full of hateful fantasies.
Take thou some of it, and seek through this grove:
A sweet Athenian lady is in love   260
With a disdainful youth: anoint his eyes –
But do it when the next thing he espies
May be the lady. Thou shalt know the man
By the Athenian garments he hath on.
Effect it with some care; that he may prove
More fond on her than she upon her love: [266]
And look thou meet me ere the first cock crow.

Puck Fear not, my lord: your servant shall do so.   *Exeunt*

Scene 2

Another part of the wood

Titania lies couched in her bower beneath the bank,
her fairies attending her

Titania Come, now a roundel and a fairy song:
Then, for the third part of a minute, hence –
Some to kill cankers in the musk-rose buds,
Some war with rere-mice for their leathern wings,
To make my small elves coats, and some keep back
The clamorous owl, that nightly hoots and wonders
At our quaint spirits. Sing me now asleep;
Then to your offices, and let me rest.

Fairies sing:

You spotted snakes, with double tongue,
Thorny hedgehogs be not seen,   10
Newts and blind-worms do no wrong,
Come not near our Fairy Queen.
Philomel, with melody,

---

255 **throws:** sheds
256 **weed:** clothing
262 **espies:** catches sight of

1 **roundel:** circle dance
3 **cankers:** canker-worm
4 **rere-mice:** bats

35

Titania to Cobweb:
   ". . . Sing me now asleep;
   Then to your offices, and let me rest."

Sing in our sweet lullaby,
  Lulla, lulla, lullaby,
  Lulla, lulla, lullaby,
  Never harm,   [17-20]
  Nor spell, nor charm,
Come our lovely lady nigh.
So good night, with lullaby.   20

1st Fairy   Weaving spiders come not here:
  Hence you long-legged spinners, hence:
Beetles black approach not near:
  Worm nor snail do no offence.
Philomel, with melody,   [25-28]
Sing in our sweet lullaby,
  Lulla, lulla, lullaby,
  Lulla, lulla, lullaby,
  Never harm
  Nor spell, nor charm,   30
Come our lovely lady nigh.
So good night, with lullaby.   *Titania sleeps*

2nd Fairy   Hence, away: now all is well:
One aloof stand sentinel.

The fairies steal away [Scene 11]

Enter Oberon

He anoints the eyes of Titania with the juice of the flower

Oberon   What thou see'st when thou dost wake,
Do it for thy true-love take;
Love and languish for his sake.
Be it ounce, or cat, or bear,
Pard, or boar with bristled hair,
In thy eye that shall appear   40
When thou wak'st, it is thy dear:
Wake, when some vile thing is near.   *Exit*

Enter Lysander with Hermia leaning upon his arm

Lysander   Fair love, you faint with wandring in the wood:
And to speak troth I have forgot our way.
We'll rest us, Hermia, if you think it good,
And tarry for the comfort of the day.

Hermia   Be 't so, Lysander: Find you out a bed:
For I upon this bank will rest my head.

Lysander   One turf shall serve as pillow for us both,

---

38 **ounce:** lynx
39 **pard:** panther
46 **tarry:** wait

Lysander: "One turf shall serve as pillow for us both,
     One heart, one bed, two bosoms, and one troth."
Hermia: "Nay, good Lysander: for my sake, my dear,
     Lie further off yer; do not lie so near.

	One heart, one bed, two bosoms, and one troth.	50
Hermia	Nay, good Lysander: for my sake, my dear,
	Lie further off yet; do not lie so near.
Lysander	O take the sense, sweet, of my innocence!
	Love takes the meaning in love's conference.
	I mean that my heart unto yours is knit;
	So that but one heart we can make of it:
	Two bosoms interchainéd with an oath:
	So then two bosoms and a single troth.
	Then by your side no bed-room me deny:
	For, lying so, Hermia, I do not lie.	60
Hermia	Lysander riddles very prettily.
	Now much beshrew my manners and my pride,
	If Hermia meant to say Lysander lied.
	But, gentle friend, for love and courtesy
	Lie further off – in human modesty:
	Such separation as may well be said
	Becomes a virtuous bachelor and a maid,
	So far be distant – and good night, sweet friend:
	Thy love ne'er alter till thy sweet life end!
Lysander	Amen, amen, to that fair prayer, say I –	70
	And then end life when I end loyalty.
	Here is my bed: sleep give thee all his rest.
Hermia	With half that wish the wisher's eyes be pressed.

They sleep

Enter Puck

Puck	Through the forest have I gone,
	But Athenian found I none,
	On whose eyes I might approve
	This flower's force in stirring love.
	Night and silence – Who is here?
	Weeds of Athens he doth wear:
	This is he, my master said,	80
	Despiséd the Athenian maid:
	And here the maiden, sleeping sound,
	On the dank and dirty ground.
	Pretty soul, she durst not lie
	Near this lack-love, this kill-courtesy.

He anoints the eyelids of Lysander

| | Churl, upon thy eyes I throw |
| | All the power this charm doth owe: |

---

50 **troth:** truth
76 **approve:** test
86 **churl:** boor

When thou wak'st, let love forbid
Sleep his seat on thy eyelid.
So awake when I am gone: 90
For I must now to Oberon   *Exit*

Enter Demetrius and Helena, running

Helena	Stay; though thou kill me, sweet Demetrius.
Demetrius	I charge thee, hence, and do not haunt me thus.
Helena	O, wilt thou darkling leave me? Do not so.
Demetrius	Stay, on thy peril; I alone will go. *Exit*
Helena	O, I am out of breath in this fond chase.

           The more my prayer, the lesser is my grace.
           Happy is Hermia, wheresoe'er she lies;
           For she hath blessèd and attractive eyes.
           How came her eyes so bright? Not with salt tears –   100
           If so, my eyes are oft'ner washed than hers.
           No, no: I am as ugly as a bear;
           For beasts that meet me run away for fear.
           Therefore no marvel though Demetrius
           Do, as a monster, fly my presence thus.
           What wicked and dissembling glass of mine
           Made me compare with Hermia's sphery eyne?
           But who is here? Lysander! On the ground!
           Dead? Or asleep? I see no blood, no wound.
           Lysander, if you live, good sir, awake.   110

Lysander	*(leaps ups)* And run through fire I will, for thy sweet sake.

           Transparent Helena! Nature shows art   [112]
           That through my bosom makes me see thy heart.
           Where is Demetrius? O, how fit a word
           Is that vile name to perish on my sword!

Helena	Do not say so, Lysander, say not so.

           What though he love your Hermia? Lord! What though?
           Yet Hermia still loves you: then be content.

Lysander	Content with Hermia? No: I do repent

           The tedious minutes I with her have spent.   120
           Not Hermia, but Helena I love –
           Who will not change a raven for a dove?
           The will of man is by his reason swayed;
           And reason says you are the worthier maid.
           Things growing are not ripe until their season:
           So I, being young, till now ripe not to reason –
           And touching now the point of human skill,

---

94 **darkling:** in the dark
106 **dissembling glass:** mirror that alters appearance
107 **sphery eyne:** starlike eyes

HELENA.
WEDDING.
ROSEMARY DINSMORE

A MIDSUMMER NIGHTS DREAM.   STRATFORD ON.

	Reason becomes the marshal to my will,	
	And leads me to your eyes; where I o'erlook	
	Love's stories, written in love's richest book.	130
Helena	Wherefore was I to this keen mockery born?	
	When at your hands did I deserve this scorn?	
	Is 't not enough, is 't not enough, young man,	
	That I did never, no, nor never can,	
	Deserve a sweet look from Demetrius' eye,	
	But you must flout my insufficiency?	
	Good troth you do me wrong, good sooth you do,	
	In such disdainful manner me to woo.	
	But fare you well: perforce I must confess	
	I thought you lord of more true gentleness.	140
	O, that a lady, of one man refused,	
	Should of another therefore be abused!	*Exit*
Lysander	She sees not Hermia. Hermia, sleep thou there,	
	And never mayst thou come Lysander near.	
	For, as a surfeit of the sweetest things	
	The deepest loathing to the stomach brings:	
	Or as the heresies that men do leave	
	Are hated most of those they did deceive;	
	So thou, my surfeit and my heresy,	
	Of all be hated; but the most of me!	150
	And all my powers, address your love and might,	
	To honour Helen, and to be her knight.	*Exit*
Hermia	*(awaking)* Help me, Lysander, help me! Do thy best	
	To pluck this crawling serpent from my breast.	
	Ay me, for pity! What a dream was here?	
	Lysander, look how I do quake with fear.	
	Methought a serpent eat my heart away,	
	And you sat smiling at his cruel prey.	
	Lysander! What, removed? – Lysander! Lord!	
	What, out of hearing? Gone? No sound, no word?	160
	Alack, where are you? Speak, an if you hear;	
	Speak, of all loves! I swoon almost with fear.	
	No? Then I well perceive you are not nigh:	
	Either death or you I'll find immediately.	*Exit*

---

128 **will**: desire
129 **o'erlook**: read (look over)
136 **flout**: mock
137 **troth**: faith   **sooth**: truth

145 **surfeit**: excess
161 **an if**: if
162 **of all loves**: for love's sake

Scene 1

[Scene 12]

Enter Quince (carrying a bag), Snug, Bottom,
Flute, Snout, and Starveling

Bottom	Are we all met?
Quince	Pat, pat: and here's a marvellous convenient place
	for our rehearsal. This green plot shall be our stage,
	this hawthorn-brake our tiring-house – and we will
	do it in action as we will do it before the duke.
Bottom	Peter Quince!
Quince	What sayst thou, bully Bottom?
Bottom	There are things in this comedy of Pyramus and
	Thisbe that will never please. First, Pyramus must draw
	a sword to kill himself; which the ladies cannot abide. 10
	How answer you that?
Snout	By'r lakin, a parlous fear.
Starveling	I believe we must leave the killing out,
	when all is done.
Bottom	Not a whit: I have a device to make all well.
	Write me a prologue, and let the prologue seem
	to say we will do no harm with our swords, and that
	Pyramus is not killed indeed: and, for the more better
	assurance, tell them that I, Pyramus, am not Pyramus,
	but Bottom the weaver: this will put them out of fear. 20
Quince	Well: we will have such a prologue,
	and it shall be written in eight and six. [22]
Bottom	No: make it two more: let it be
	written in eight and eight.

---

  2 **Pat:** on the dot
  4 **tiring-house:** attiring house (dressing-room)
12 **By'r lakin:** by our Lady
    parlous: perilous

Bottom to Flute, played by Simon Bradbury, Quince, Starveling, and Snout:
"There are things in this comedy of Pyramus and
Thisbe that will never please. First, Pyramus must draw
a sword to kill himself; which the ladies cannot abide."

Snout	Will not the ladies be afeard of the lion?
Starveling	I fear it, I promise you.
Bottom	Masters, you ought to consider with yourselves
	– to bring in – God shield us – a lion among ladies, is a
	most dreadful thing. For there is not a more fearful
	wild-fowl than your lion living; and we ought to look to 't. 30
Snout	Therefore, another prologue must tell he
	is not a lion.
Bottom	Nay: you must name his name, and half his face
	must be seen through the lion's neck, and he
	himself must speak through, saying thus, or to the same
	defect; 'Ladies,' or 'Fair ladies – I would wish you,'
	or 'I would request you,' or 'I would entreat you,
	not to fear, not to tremble: my life for yours. If you
	think I come hither as a lion, it were pity of my life.
	No: I am no such thing: I am a man as other
	men are': and there, indeed, let him name his name, 40
	and tell them plainly he is Snug the joiner.
Quince	Well; it shall be so. But there is two hard things:
	that is, to bring the moonlight into a chamber:
	for you know, Pyramus and Thisbe meet by moonlight.
Snout	Doth the moon shine that night we play our play?
Bottom	A calendar, a calendar! Look in the almanac
	– find out moonshine, find out moonshine.
Quince	Yes: it doth shine that night.
Bottom	Why, then may you leave a casement of the 50
	great chamber window, where we play, open;
	and the moon may shine in at the casement.
Quince	Ay; or else one must come in with a bush of [53-54]
	thorns and a lanthorn, and say he comes to
	disfigure, or to present, the person of Moonshine.
	Then, there is another thing: we must have a
	wall of the great chamber; for Pyramus and Thisbe,
	says the story, did talk through the chink of a wall.
Snout	You can never bring in a wall. What say you, Bottom?
Bottom	Some man or other must present wall: and let him 60
	have some plaster, or some loam, or some rough-
	cast about him, to signify wall; and let him hold his
	fingers thus – *(he stretches out his fingers)* and through
	that cranny shall Pyramus and Thisbe whisper.
Quince	If that may be, then all is well. Come, sit down,
	every mother's son, and rehearse your parts.
	Pyramus, you begin: when you have spoken

---

50 **casement**: window-frame

your speech, enter into that brake – and so
every one according to his cue.

Puck appears

Puck	What hempen homespuns have we swagg'ring here,	70
	So near the cradle of the Fairy Queen?	
	What, a play toward? I'll be an auditor,	
	An actor too perhaps, if I see cause.	
Quince	Speak, Pyramus. Thisbe, stand forth.	
Bottom	'Thisbe, the flowers ha' odious savours sweet,' –	
Quince	*(prompts)* Odorous, odorous.	
Bottom	– odours savours sweet,	[77]
	So hath thy breath, my dearest Thisbe dear.	
	But hark, a voice: stay thou but here awhile,	
	And by and by I will to thee appear.'	80

                                                   Exit

Puck	A stranger Pyramus than e'er played here!	*Exit*
Flute	Must I speak now?	
Quince	Ay, marry, must you. For you must	
	understand he goes but to see a noise	
	that he heard, and is to come again.	
Flute	'Most radiant Pyramus, most lily-white of hue,	
	Of colour like the red rose on triumphant briar,	
	Most brisky juvenal, and eke most lovely Jew,	
	As true as truest horse that yet would never tire,	
	I'll meet thee, Pyramus, at Ninny's tomb.'	[90]
Quince	'Ninus' tomb,' man! Why, you must not	
	speak that yet! That you answer to Pyramus.	
	You speak all your part at once, cues and all.	
	Pyramus enter; your cue is past; it is, 'never tire.'	
Flute	O. – 'As true as truest horse, that yet would never tire.'	

Enter Bottom with an ass's head, Puck following

Bottom	'If I were fair, Thisbe, I were only thine.'
Quince	O monstrous! O strange! We are haunted.
	Pray masters, fly masters! Help!

                                   They all run away and hide in the bushes

Puck	I'll follow you: I'll lead you about a round,	
	Thorough bog, thorough bush, thorough brake,	100
	Thorough briar;	
	Sometime a horse I'll be, sometime a hound,	
	A hog, a headless bear, sometime a fire,	
	And neigh, and bark, and grunt, and roar, and burn,	

---

       88 brisky juvenal: swift youth

Titania to Bottom: "Thou art as wise as thou art beautiful."

Bottom Why do they run away? This is a knavery of
them to make me afeard.

Enter Snout

Snout O Bottom, thou art changed! What do I see
on thee?

Bottom What do you see? You see an ass-head of
your own, do you?   *Exit Snout* 110

Enter Quince

Quince Bless thee Bottom, bless thee! Thou art
translated.   *Exit* [Scene 13]

Bottom I see their knavery. This is to make an ass of me,
to fright me if they could: but I will not stir from this place,
do what they can. I will walk up and down here,
and will sing that they shall hear I am not afraid.

He sings:

The ousel cock, so black of hue,
   With orange-tawny bill,
The throstle with his note so true,
   The wren with little quill –   120

Titania *(comes from the bower)* What angel wakes
               me from my flow'ry bed?

Bottom The finch, the sparrow, and the lark,
   The plain-song cuckoo gray:
Whose note full many a man doth mark,
   And dares not answer, nay –
for indeed, who would set his wit to so foolish a bird? Who
would give a bird the lie, though he cry 'cuckoo' never so?

Titania I pray thee, gentle mortal, sing again!
Mine ear is much enamoured of thy note.
So is mine eye enthrallèd to thy shape,   130
And thy fair virtue's force – perforce – doth move me,
On the first view, to say, to swear, I love thee.

Bottom Methinks, mistress, you should have little reason for
that. And yet, to say the truth, reason and love keep
little company together now-a-days. The more the pity,
that some honest neighbours will not make them friends. [136]
Nay, I can gleek upon occasion.

---

117 **ousel cock:** male blackbird
119 **throstle:** thrush
123 **plain-song:** having a simple song
126 **set his wit:** use his wit to answer
137 **gleek:** make a satirical joke

TITANIA FAIRIES.
J. MCDONALD.

HEELEY 84

A MIDSUMMER NIGHTS DREAM, STRATFORD ONTARIO

Titania	Thou art as wise as thou art beautiful.
Bottom	Not so, neither: but if I had wit enough to get out
	of this wood, I have enough to serve mine own turn. 140
Titania	Out of this wood do not desire to go:
	Thou shalt remain here, whether thou wilt or no.
	I am a spirit of no common rate:
	The summer still doth tend upon my state,
	And I do love thee: therefore go with me.
	I'll give thee fairies to attend on thee:
	And they shall fetch thee jewels from the deep,
	And sing, while thou on pressèd flowers dost sleep:
	And I will purge thy mortal grossness so,
	That thou shalt like an airy spirit go. 150
	Peaseblossom, Cobweb, Moth, and Mustardseed! [151]
Peaseblossom	Ready!
Cobweb	And I –
Moth	And I –
Mustardseed	And I –
All	*bowing* Where shall we go?
Titania	Be kind and courteous to this gentleman,
	Hop in his walks and gambol in his eyes,
	Feed him with apricocks and dewberries,
	With purple grapes, green figs, and mulberries.
	The honey-bags steal from the humble-bees,
	And for night-tapers crop their waxen thighs,
	And light them at the fiery glow-worm's eyes,
	To have my love to bed and to rise, 160
	And pluck the wings from painted butterflies,
	To fan the moonbeams from his sleeping eyes.
	Nod to him, elves, and do him courtesies.
Peaseblossom	Hail, mortal!
Cobweb	Hail!
Moth	Hail!
Mustardseed	Hail!
Bottom	I cry your worships mercy, heartily.
	I beseech your worship's name.
Cobweb	Cobweb. 170
Bottom	I shall desire you of more acquaintance, good
	Master Cobweb: If I cut my finger, I shall make bold
	with you. Your name, honest gentleman? [173]
Peaseblossom	Peaseblossom.

---

155 **apricocks:** apricots
     dewberries: form of blackberries

Bottom	I pray you, commend me to Mistress Squash,
	your mother, and to Master Peascod, your father.
	Good Master Peaseblossom, I shall desire you of more [177]
	acquaintance too. Your name, I beseech you, sir?
Mustardseed	Mustardseed.
Bottom	Good Master Mustardseed, I know your 180
	patience well. That same cowardly, giant-like, Oxbeef
	hath devoured many a gentleman of your house. I
	promise you, your kindred hath made my eyes water
	ere now. I desire you of more acquaintance, good
	Master Mustardseed.
Titania	Come, wait upon him; lead him to my bower.
	The moon, methinks, looks with a wat'ry eye: [187]
	And when she weeps, weeps every little flower,
	Lamenting some enforcéd chastity. [189]
	Tie up my love's tongue, bring him silently. 190

Exeunt

INTERVAL

Scene 2

[Scene 14]

Enter Oberon

Oberon	I wonder if Titania be awaked;
	Then, what it was that next came in her eye,
	Which she must dote on in extremity.

Enter Puck

	Here comes my messenger. How now, mad spirit?
	What night-rule now about this haunted grove?
Puck	My mistress with a monster is in love.
	Near to her close and consecrated bower,
	While she was in her dull and sleeping hour,
	A crew of patches, rude mechanicals,
	That work for bread upon Athenian stalls, 10
	Were met together to rehearse a play
	Intended for great Theseus' nuptial-day.
	The shallowest thick-skin of that barren sort,

---

175 **Squash:** unripe pea pod
176 **Peascod:** ripe pea pod
  5 **night-rule:** revels

7 **close:** secret
9 **patches:** fools
  rude mechanicals: rough working men

Who Pyramus presented, in their sport
Forsook his scene and entred in a brake,
When I did him at this advantage take:
An ass's noll I fixéd on his head.
Anon his Thisbe must be answeréd,
And forth my mimic comes. When they him spy –
As wild geese that the creeping fowler eye,   20
Or russet-pated choughs, many in sort,
Rising and cawing at the gun's report,
Sever themselves, and madly sweep the sky.
So, at his sight, away his fellows fly;
And at our stamp here o'er and o'er one falls –
He 'murder' cries, and help from Athens calls.
Their sense thus weak, lost with their fears thus strong,
Made senseless things begin to do them wrong.
For briars and thorns at their apparel snatch:
Some sleeves, some hats; from yielders all things catch.   30
I led them on in this distracted fear,
And left sweet Pyramus translated there:
When in that moment – so it came to pass –
Titania waked and straightway loved an ass.

Oberon   This falls out better than I could devise.
But hast thou yet latched the Athenian's eyes
With the love-juice, as I did bid thee do?

Puck   I took him sleeping – that is finished too –
And the Athenian woman by his side;
That, when he waked, of force she must be eyed.   40

Enter Demetrius and Hermia

Oberon   Stand close; this is the same Athenian.   [Scene 15]
Puck   This is the woman: but not this the man.
Demetrius   O, why rebuke you him that loves you so?
Lay breath so bitter on your bitter foe.
Hermia   Now I but chide: but I should use thee worse,
For thou, I fear, hast given me cause to curse.
If thou hast slain Lysander in his sleep,
Being o'er-shoes in blood, plunge in the deep,
And kill me too.
The sun was not so true unto the day   50
As he to me. Would he have stolen away
From sleeping Hermia? I'll believe as soon

---

17 **noll:** head
21 **chough:** jackdaw (bird)
36 **latched:** fastened, or moistened (rare)
48 **o'ershoes:** over your shoes (so deep)

Oberon: "Here comes my messenger. How now, mad spirit?"

	This whole earth may be bored, and that the moon	
	May through the centre creep, and so displease	
	Her brother's noontide with th' Antipodes.	
	It cannot be but thou hast murdred him –	
	So should a murderer look; so dead, so grim.	
Demetrius	So should the murdered look, and so should I,	
	Pierced through the heart with your stern cruelty.	
	Yet you, the murderer, look as bright, as clear,	
	As yonder Venus in her glimmering sphere.	60
Hermia	What's this to my Lysander? Where is he?	
	Ah, good Demetrius, wilt thou give him me?	
Demetrius	I had rather give his carcass to my hounds.	
Hermia	Out, dog! Out, cur! Thou driv'st me past the bounds	
	Of maiden's patience. Hast thou slain him then?	
	Henceforth be never numbred among men.	
	O, once tell true: tell true, even for my sake:	
	Durst thou have looked upon him being awake?	
	And hast thou killed him, sleeping? O brave touch!	70
	Could not a worm, an adder, do so much?	
	An adder did it; for with doubler tongue	
	Than thine, thou serpent, never adder stung.	
Demetrius	You spend your passion on a misprized mood:	
	I am not guilty of Lysander's blood;	
	Nor is he dead, for aught that I can tell.	
Hermia	I pray thee, tell me then that he is well.	
Demetrius	An if I could, what should I get therefore?	
Hermia	A privilege, never to see me more.	
	And from thy hated presence part I so:	80
	See me no more, whether he be dead or no.	*Exit*
Demetrius	There is no following her in this fierce vein.	
	Here therefore a while I will remain.	
	So sorrow's heaviness doth heavier grow	
	For debt that bankrupt sleep doth sorrow owe;	
	Which now in some slight measure it will pay,	
	If for his tender here I make some stay.	[Scene 16]

He lies down

Oberon	What hast thou done? Thou hast mistaken quite,	
	And laid the love-juice on some true-love's sight.	
	Of thy misprision must perforce ensue	90
	Some true love turned, and not a false turned true.	
Puck	Then fate o'er-rules, that, one man holding troth,	

---

55 **Her brother:** i.e., the sun
th' Antipodes: the other side of the earth
71 **worm:** serpent

74 **misprized mood:** anger based on misunderstanding
78 **An if:** even if
90 **misprision:** mistaking

Oberon, bending over the sleeping Demetrius:
  "Flower of this purple dye,
  Hit with Cupid's archery,
    Sink in apple of his eye."

	A million fail, confounding oath on oath.	
Oberon	About the wood go swifter than the wind,	
	And Helena of Athens look thou find.	
	All fancy-sick she is, and pale of cheer	
	With sighs of love that costs the fresh blood dear.	
	By some illusion see thou bring her here:	
	I'll charm his eyes against she do appear.	
Puck	I go, I go – look how I go –	100
	Swifter than arrow from the Tartar's bow. *Exit*	

Oberon bends over the sleeping Demetrius

Oberon   Flower of this purple dye,
              Hit with Cupid's archery,
              Sink in apple of his eye.
              When his love he doth espy,
              Let her shine as gloriously
              As the Venus of the sky.
              When thou wak'st, if she be by,
              Beg of her for remedy.

Re-enter Puck

Puck   Captain of our fairy band,   110
              Helena is here at hand,
              And the youth, mistook by me,
              Pleading for a lover's fee.
              Shall we their fond pageant see?
              Lord, what fools these mortals be!
Oberon   Stand aside. The noise they make
              Will cause Demetrius to awake.
Puck   Then will two at once woo one;
              That must needs be sport alone.
              And those things do best please me   120
              That befall prepostrously.   *They stand aside*

Enter Helena, followed by Lysander   [Scene 17]

Lysander   Why should you think that I should woo in scorn?
                  Scorn and derision never come in tears.
              Look, when I vow, I weep; and vows so born,
                  In their nativity all truth appears.
              How can these things in me seem scorn to you,
              Bearing the badge of faith to prove them true?

---

96 **fancy-sick:** lovesick
99 **against:** ready for when
114 **fond pageant:** silly spectacle
127 **badge of faith:** tears

Helena	You do advance your cunning more and more.
	When truth kills truth, O devilish-holy fray!
	These vows are Hermia's – will you give her o'er? 130
	Weigh oath with oath, and you will nothing weigh.
	Your vows, to her and me, put in two scales,
	Will even weigh: and both as light as tales.
Lysander	I had no judgement when to her I swore.
Helena	Nor none, in my mind, now you give her o'er.
Lysander	Demetrius loves her: and he loves not you.
Demetrius	*(awaking)* O Helen, goddess, nymph, perfect, divine!
	To what, my love, shall I compare thine eyne?
	Crystal is muddy. O, how ripe in show
	Thy lips, those kissing cherries, tempting grow! 140
	That pure congealéd white, high Taurus' snow,
	Fanned with the eastern wind, turns to a crow,
	When thou hold'st up thy hand. O let me kiss
	This princess of pure white, this seal of bliss!
Helena	O spite! O hell! I see you all are bent
	To set against me for your merriment.
	If you were civil and knew courtesy,
	You would not do me thus much injury.
	Can you not hate me, as I know you do,
	But you must join in souls to mock me too? 150
	If you were men, as men you are in show,
	You would not use a gentle lady so;
	To vow, and swear, and superpraise my parts,
	When I am sure you hate me with your hearts.
	You both are rivals, and love Hermia:
	And now both rivals, to mock Helena.
	A trim exploit, a manly enterprise,
	To conjure tears up in a poor maid's eyes
	With your derision! None of noble sort
	Would so offend a virgin, and extort 160
	A poor soul's patience, all to make you sport.
Lysander	You are unkind, Demetrius; be not so –
	For you love Hermia; this you know I know;
	And here, with all good will, with all my heart,
	In Hermia's love I yield you up my part:
	And yours of Helena to me bequeath.
	Whom I do love, and will do till my death.
Helena	Never did mockers waste more idle breath.

---

141 **Taurus:** Turkish mountain range
157 **trim:** fine

Demetrius (right) to Lysander: "... keep thy Hermia: I will none.
If e'er I loved her, all that love is gone."

Demetrius	Lysander, keep thy Hermia: I will none.
	If e'er I loved her, all that love is gone. 170
	My heart to her but as guest-wise sojourned,
	And now to Helen is it home returned,
	There to remain.
Lysander	Helen, it is not so.
Demetrius	Disparage not the faith thou dost not know,
	Lest to thy peril thou aby it dear.

Enter Hermia

Look where thy love comes: yonder is thy dear.

Hermia spies Lysander and runs towards him

Hermia	Dark night, that from the eye his function takes,
	The ear more quick of apprehension makes.
	Wherein it doth impair the seeing sense,
	It pays the hearing double recompense. 180
	Thou art not by mine eye, Lysander, found;
	Mine ear, I thank it, brought me to thy sound.
	But why unkindly didst thou leave me so?
Lysander	*(turning away)* Why should he stay, whom love doth press to go?
Hermia	What love could press Lysander from my side?
Lysander	Lysander's love, that would not let him bide –
	Fair Helena! Who more engilds the night
	Than all yon fiery oes and eyes of light.
	Why seek'st thou me? Could not this make thee know,
	The hate I bear thee made me leave thee so? 190
Hermia	You speak not as you think: it cannot be.
Helena	Lo, she is one of this confederacy.
	Now I perceive they have conjoined all three
	To fashion this false sport in spite of me.
	Injurious Hermia, most ungrateful maid,
	Have you conspired, have you with these contrived
	To bait me with this foul derision?
	Is all the counsel that we two have shared,
	The sisters' vows, the hours that we have spent,
	When we have chid the hasty-footed time 200
	For parting us. O! Is all forgot?
	All school-days' friendship, childhood innocence?
	We, Hermia, like two artificial gods,
	Have with our needles created both one flower,

175 **aby it:** atone for it
186 **bide:** wait
188 **oes and eyes:** stars
197 **bait:** torment

	Both on one sampler, sitting on one cushion,	
	Both warbling of one song, both in one key;	
	As if our hands, our sides, voices, and minds,	
	Had been incorporate. So we grew together,	
	Like to a double cherry, seeming parted;	
	But yet an union in partition,	210
	Two lovely berries moulded on one stem:	
	So, with two seeming bodies, but one heart,	
	Two of the first, like coats in heraldry,	
	Due but to one, and crownéd with one crest.	
	And will you rend our ancient love asunder,	
	To join with men in scorning your poor friend?	
	It is not friendly, 'tis not maidenly –	
	Our sex, as well as I, may chide you for it;	
	Though I alone do feel the injury.	
Hermia	I am amazéd at your words.	220
Helena	I scorn you not – it seems that you scorn me.	
	Have you not set Lysander, as in scorn,	
	To follow me and praise my eyes and face?	
	And made your other love, Demetrius –	
	Who even but now did spurn me with his foot! –	
	To call me goddess, nymph, divine and rare,	
	Precious, celestial? Wherefore speaks he this	
	To her he hates? And wherefore doth Lysander	
	Deny your love – so rich within his soul –	
	And tender me forsooth affection,	230
	But by your setting on, by your consent?	
	What though I be not so in grace as you,	
	So hung upon with love, so fortunate,	
	But miserable most to love unloved?	
	This you should pity rather than despise.	
Hermia	I understand not what you mean by this.	
Helena	Ay, do! Persévér, counterfeit sad looks.	
	Make mouths upon me when I turn my back.	
	Wink at each other, hold the sweet jest up.	
	This sport, well carried, shall be chronicled.	240
	If you have any pity, grace, or manners,	
	You would not make me such an argument.	
	But, fare you well: 'tis partly my own fault:	
	Which death or absence soon shall remedy.	
Lysander	Stay, gentle Helena; hear my excuse,	
	My love, my life, my soul, fair Helena!	

---

208 **incorporate:** of one body
237 **Persévér:** persevere
242 **an argument:** subject of joking

Hermia: "I am amazéd at your words.
I scorn you not – it seems that you scorn me."

Helena	O excellent!
Hermia	Sweet, do not scorn her so.
Demetrius	If she cannot entreat, I can compel.
Lysander	Thou canst compel no more than she entreat.

Thy threats have no more strength than her   250
   weak prayers.
Helen, I love thee – by my life I do;
I swear by that which I will lose for thee,
To prove him false that says I love thee not.

Demetrius	I say I love thee more than he can do.
Lysander	If thou say so, withdraw, and prove it too.
Demetrius	Quick, come, –
Hermia	Lysander, whereto tends all this?
Lysander	Away, you Ethiop!
Demetrius	No, no: he'll

Seem to break loose! Take on, as you would follow.
But yet come not. You are a tame man, go!

Lysander   Hang off, thou cat, thou burr! Vile thing, let loose;   260
Or I will shake thee from me like a serpent.

Hermia   Why are you grown so rude? What change is this,
Sweet love?   *She keeps her hold upon him*

Lysander   Thy love! Out, tawny Tartar, out.
Out, loathéd med'cine. O, hated potion, hence!

Hermia	Do you not jest?
Helena	Yes, sooth: and so do you.
Lysander	Demetrius, I will keep my word with thee.
Demetrius	I would I had your bond, for I perceive

A weak bond holds you. I'll not trust your word.

Lysander   What? Should I hurt her, strike her, kill her dead?
Although I hate her, I'll not harm her so.   270

Hermia   What? Can you do me greater harm than hate?
Hate me, wherefore? O me, what news, my love!
Am not I Hermia? Are not you Lysander?
I am as fair now as I was erewhile.
Since night you loved me; yet, since night you left me.
Why then, you left me, – O, the gods forbid! –
In earnest, shall I say?

Lysander   Ay, by my life:
And never did desire to see thee more.
Therefore be out of hope, of question, doubt:
Be certain: nothing truer: 'tis no jest,   280
That I do hate thee and love Helena.

---

274 **erewhile:** before

Hermia	*(to Helena)* O me, you juggler, you canker-blossom,
	You thief of love! What, have you come by night
	And stol'n my love's heart from him?
Helena	Fine, i' faith!
	Have you no modesty, no maiden shame,
	No touch of bashfulness? What, will you tear
	Impatient answers from my gentle tongue?
	Fie, fie, you counterfeit, you puppet you!
Hermia	Puppet? Why so? Ay, that way goes the game.
	Now I perceive that she hath made compare
	Between our statures, she hath urged her height,
	And with her personage, her tall personage,
	Her height, forsooth, she hath prevailed with him.
	And are you grown so high in his esteem,
	Because I am so dwarfish and so low?
	How low am I, thou painted maypole? Speak;
	How low am I? I am not yet so low,
	But that my nails can reach unto thine eyes.
Helena	I pray you, though you mock me, gentlemen,
	Let her not hurt me. I was never curst:
	I have no gift at all in shrewishness:
	I am a right maid for my cowardice:
	Let her not strike me. You perhaps may think,
	Because she is something lower than myself,
	That I can match her.
Hermia	Lower! Hark, again.
Helena	Good Hermia, do not be so bitter with me.
	I evermore did love you, Hermia,
	Did ever keep your counsels, never wronged you;
	Save that, in love unto Demetrius,
	I told him of your stealth unto this wood,
	He followed you; for love I followed him.
	But he hath chid me hence, and threat'ned me
	To strike me, spurn me; nay to kill me too.
	And now, so you will let me quiet go,
	To Athens will I bear my folly back,
	And follow you no further. Let me go.
	You see how simple and how fond I am.
Hermia	Why, get you gone. Who is 't that hinders you?
Helena	A foolish heart, that I leave here behind.
Hermia	What, with Lysander?
Helena	With Demetrius.
Lysander	Be not afraid: she shall not harm thee, Helena.

290

300

310

320

---

282 **canker-blossom:** worm that cankers the blossom
300 **curst:** shrewish

Helena (right) as Lysander and Demetrius hold Hermia:
"Have you no modesty, no maiden shame,
No touch of bashfulness? What, will you tear
Impatient answers from my gentle tongue?"

Demetrius	No, sir; she shall not, though you take her part.
Helena	When she is angry, she is keen and shrewd.
	She was a vixen when she went to school;
	And though she be but little, she is fierce.
Hermia	'Little' again? Nothing but 'low' and 'little'!
	Why will you suffer her to flout me thus?
	Let me come to her.
Lysander	Get you gone, you dwarf;
	You minimus, of hindring knot-grass made;
	You bead, you acorn.
Demetrius	You are too officious
	In her behalf that scorns your services.
	Let her alone; speak not of Helena –
	Take not her part *(he draws his sword)* for if thou dost intend
	Never so little show of love to her,
	Thou shalt aby it.
Lysander	*(also draws)* Now she holds me not;
	Now follow, if thou dar'st, to try whose right,
	Of thine or mine, is most in Helena. *Exit*
Demetrius	Follow! Nay, I'll go with thee, cheek by jowl. *Exit*
Hermia	You, mistress, all this coil is 'long of you:
	Nay: go not back.
Helena	I will not trust you, I,
	Nor longer stay in your curst company.
	Your hands than mine are quicker for a fray;
	My legs are longer though to run away. *Exit*
Hermia	I am amazed, and know not what to say. *Exit*
Oberon	*(advancing)* This is thy negligence: still thou mistak'st, [Scene 18]
	Or else committ'st thy knaveries wilfully.
Puck	Believe me, king of shadows, I mistook.
	Did not you tell me I should know the man
	By the Athenian garments he had on?
	And so far blameless proves my enterprise,
	That I have 'nointed an Athenian's eyes:
	And so far am I glad it so did sort,
	As this their jangling I esteem a sport.
Oberon	Thou see'st these lovers seek a place to fight:
	Hie therefore, Robin, overcast the night,
	The starry welkin cover thou anon
	With drooping fog as black as Acheron,

330

340

350

356

357

---

329 **minimus:** tiny creature
knot-grass: low weed, the juice of which supposedly stunted growth
351 **'nointed:** annointed
356 **welkin:** sky
357 **Acheron:** river of hell

And lead these testy rivals so astray,
As one come not within another's way.
Like to Lysander sometime frame thy tongue;   360
Then stir Demetrius up with bitter wrong;
And sometime rail thou like Demetrius:
And from each other look thou lead them thus,
Till o'er their brows death-counterfeiting sleep
With leaden legs and batty wings doth creep:
Then crush this herb into Lysander's eye;
Whose liquor hath this virtuous property,
To take from thence all error with his might,
And make his eyeballs roll with wonted sight.
When they next wake, all this derision   370
Shall seem a dream and fruitless vision,
And back to Athens shall the lovers wend,
With league whose date till death shall never end.
Whiles I in this affair do thee employ,
I'll to my queen and beg her Indian boy;
And then I will her charméd eye release
From monster's view, and all things shall be peace.

Puck   My fairy lord, this must be done with haste,
For night's swift dragons cut the clouds full fast,
And yonder shines Aurora's harbinger;   380
At whose approach, ghosts, wandring here and there,
Troop home to churchyards: damnéd spirits all,
That in crossways and floods have burial,
Already to their wormy beds are gone;
For fear lest day should look their shames upon,
They wilfully themselves exile from light,
And must for aye consort with black-browed night.

Oberon   But we are spirits of another sort,
I with the morning's love have oft made sport,
And like a forester the groves may tread,   390
Even till the eastern gate, all fiery-red,
Opening on Neptune with fair blesséd beams,
Turns into yellow gold his salt green streams.
But, notwithstanding, haste – make no delay:
We may effect this business yet ere day.   *Exit*

A fog descends

---

365 **batty:** batlike
367 **virtuous:** potent
380 **Aurora's harbinger:** morning star
383 **crossways:** suicides were buried at crossroads
    floods: drowned souls could not rest because no burial rites had been performed
389 **morning's love:** Aurora
392 **Neptune:** the ocean

Puck	Up and down, up and down,
	I will lead them up and down.
	I am feared in field and town.
	Goblin, lead them up and down.
	Here comes one. 400

Re-enter Lysander   [Scene 19]

Lysander	Where art thou, proud Demetrius? Speak thou now.
Puck	*(in Demetrius's voice)* Here villain! Drawn and
	ready. Where art thou?
Lysander	I will be with thee straight.
Puck	Follow me then
	To plainer ground. *Exit Lysander* [404]

Re-enter Demetrius

Demetrius	Lysander! Speak again.
	Thou runaway, thou coward, art thou fled?
	Speak! In some bush? Where dost thou hide thy head?
Puck	*(in Lysander's voice)* Thou coward, art thou bragging to the stars,
	Telling the bushes that thou look'st for wars,
	And wilt not come? Come recreant, come thou child,
	I'll whip thee with a rod. He is defiled, 410
	That draws a sword on thee.
Demetrius	Yea, art thou there?
Puck	Follow my voice: we'll try no manhood here.
	Exit Demetrius

Re-enter Lysander

Lysander	He goes before me and still dares me on:
	When I come where he calls, then he is gone.
	The villain is much lighter-heeled than I:
	I followed fast; but faster he did fly;
	That fallen am I in dark uneven way,
	And here will rest me. *He lies down*
	Come, thou gentle day,
	For if but once thou show me thy grey light,
	I'll find Demetrius and revenge this spite. *He sleeps* 420

Demetrius returns, running

---

409 **recreant:** one who surrenders
412 **try:** test

Lysander: "The villain is much lighter-heeled than I:
    I followed fast; but faster did he fly..."

Puck	Ho, ho, ho! Coward, why com'st thou not?
Demetrius	Abide me if thou dar'st, for well I wot
	Thou runn'st before me, shifting every place,
	And dar'st not stand, nor look me in the face.
	Where art thou now?
Puck	Come hither; I am here.
Demetrius	Nay, then thou mock'st me. Thou shalt buy this dear,
	If ever I thy face by daylight see.
	Now, go thy way. Faintness constraineth me
	To measure out my length on this cold bed.
	By day's approach look to be visited.

430

He lies down and sleeps

Re-enter Helena

Helena	O weary night, O long and tedious night,
	Abate thy hours! Shine comforts from the east;
	That I may back to Athens by daylight,
	From these that my poor company detest.
	And sleep, that sometimes shuts up sorrow's eye,
	Steal me awhile from mine own company.

She lies down and sleeps

Re-enter Puck

Puck	Yet but three? Come one more.
	Two of both kinds makes up four.
	Here she comes, curst and sad.
	Cupid is a knavish lad,
	Thus to make poor females mad.

440

Re-enter Hermia

Hermia	Never so weary, never so in woe,
	Bedabbled with the dew and torn with briars;
	I can no further crawl, no further go;
	My legs can keep no pace with my desires.
	Here will I rest me until the break of day.
	Heavens shield Lysander, if they mean a fray!

She goes to sleep

Puck	On the ground
	Sleep sound:
	I'll apply
	To your eye,
	Gentle lover, remedy.

450

---

422 **wot:** know
426 **buy this dear:** pay for this
432 **Abate:** shorten

He anoints Lysander's eyes with the love-juice

> When thou wak'st,
> Thou tak'st
> True delight
> In the sight
> Of thy former lady's eye:
> And the country proverb known,
> That every man should take his own,
> In your waking shall be shown.   460
> Jack shall have Jill;
> Nought shall go ill;
> The man shall have his mare again, and all shall be well.

Exit

Act Fourth

Scene 1 [Scene 20]

Titania approaches with Bottom, his ass's head
garlanded with flowers; fairies follow in their train,
Oberon behind all, unseen

Titania	Come, sit thee down upon this flow'ry bed,
	While I thy amiable cheeks do coy,
	And stick musk-roses in thy sleek smooth head,
	And kiss thy fair large ears, my gentle joy.

They sit; she embraces him

Bottom	Where's Peaseblossom?	
Peaseblossom	Ready.	
Bottom	Scratch my head, Peaseblossom. Where's Monsieur Cobweb?	
Cobweb	Ready.	
Bottom	Monsieur Cobweb, good monsieur, get you your weapons in your hand, and kill me a red-hipped humble-bee on the top of a thistle; and, good monsieur, bring me the honey-bag. Do not fret yourself too much in the action, monsieur; and, good monsieur, have a care the honey-bag break not – I would be loath to have you overflown with a honey-bag, signior. Where's Monsieur Mustardseed?	10
Mustardseed	Ready.	
Bottom	Give me your neaf, Monsieur Mustardseed. Pray you, leave your curtsy, good monsieur.	20
Mustardseed	What's your will?	
Bottom	Nothing, good monsieur, but to help Cavalery Cobweb to scratch. I must to the barber's, monsieur, for methinks I am marvellous hairy about the face	

---

2 **coy:** caress   24 **marvellous:** very
19 **neuf:** fist

Bottom to Cobweb and Titania:
   "... I must to the barber's ...
   for methinks I am marvellous hairy about the face
   –and I am such a tender ass, if my hair do but
   tickle me, I must scratch."

	– and I am such a tender ass, if my hair do but	
	tickle me, I must scratch.	
Titania	What, wilt thou hear some music, my sweet love?	
Bottom	I have a reasonable good ear in music.	
	Let's have the tongs and the bones.	[29]
Titania	Or, say, sweet love, what thou desir'st to eat.	30
Bottom	Truly, a peck of provender. I could munch	
	your good dry oats. Methinks I have a great desire to	
	a bottle of hay. Good hay, sweet hay, hath no fellow.	
Titania	I have a venturous fairy, that shall seek	
	The squirrel's hoard, and fetch thee new nuts.	[35]
Bottom	I had rather have a handful or two of dried pease.	
	But, I pray you – let none of your people stir me.	
	I have an exposition of sleep upon me.	
Titania	Sleep thou, and I will wind thee in my arms.	
	Fairies, be gone, and be all ways away.	40

          Exeunt fairies

	So doth the woodbine the sweet honeysuckle	[41]
	Gently entwist: the female ivy so	
	Enrings the barky fingers of the elm.	
	O, how I love thee! How I dote on thee! *They sleep*	

Oberon comes forward   [Scene 21]

Enter Puck

Oberon	Welcome, good Robin. See'st thou this sweet sight?	
	Her dotage now I do begin to pity.	
	For meeting her of late behind the wood,	
	Seeking sweet favours for this hateful fool,	
	I did upbraid her and fall out with her:	
	For she his hairy temples then had rounded	50
	With coronet of fresh and fragrant flowers:	
	And that same dew, which sometime on the buds	
	Was wont to swell like round and orient pearls,	
	Stood now within the pretty flowerets' eyes	
	Like tears that did their own disgrace bewail.	
	When I had at my pleasure taunted her,	
	And she in mild terms begged my patience,	
	I then did ask of her her changeling child;	
	Which straight she gave me, and her fairy sent	
	To bear him to my bower in Fairyland.	60
	And now I have the boy, I will undo	
	This hateful imperfection of her eyes.	

31 **provender:** dry food (hay, corn)
33 **bottle:** small bundle
48 **favours:** flowers

And, gentle Puck, take this transforméd scalp
From off the head of this Athenian swain:
That he, awaking when the other do,
May all to Athens back again repair,
And think no more of this night's accidents,
But as the fierce vexation of a dream.
But first I will release the Fairy Queen.

    Be as thou wast wont to be: *(he anoints her eyes)* 70
    See, as thou wast wont to see.
    Dian's bud o'er Cupid's flower
    Hath such force and blesséd power.
Now, my Titania! Wake you, my sweet queen.

Titania My Oberon, what visions have I seen!
Methought I was enamoured of an ass.

Oberon There lies your love.

Titania   How came these things to pass?
O, how mine eyes do loathe his visage now!

Oberon Silence, awhile! Robin, take off his head.
Titania, music call, and strike more dead   80
Than common sleep of all these five the sense.

Titania Music, Ho! Music! Such as charmeth sleep.

Puck Now, when thou wak'st, with thine own fool's eyes peep.

He plucks the ass's head from him

Oberon Sound, music. Come, my queen, take hands with me, [84]
And rock the ground whereon these sleepers be.

                          They dance

Now thou and I are new in amity,
And will to-morrow midnight solemnly
Dance in Duke Theseus' house triumphantly,
And bless it to all fair prosperity.
There shall the pairs of faithful lovers be   90
Wedded, with Theseus, all in jollity.

Puck   Fairy King, attend and mark:
    I do hear the morning lark.

Oberon Then, my queen, in silence sad,
    Trip we after the night's shade:
    We the globe can compass soon,
    Swifter than the wandring moon.

Titania Come, my lord, and in our flight,
    Tell me how it came this night

---

86 **amity:** friendship

That I sleeping here was found   100
With these mortals on the ground.   *Exeunt*

Enter Theseus, Hippolyta, Egeus, and others arrayed for the hunt   [Scene 22]

Theseus   Go one of you, find out the forester;
For now our observation is performed,
And since we have the vaward of the day,
My love shall hear the music of my hounds.
Uncouple in the western valley, let them go:
Dispatch, I say, and find the forester.
We will, fair queen, up to the mountain's top,
And mark the musical confusion
Of hounds and echo in conjunction.   110

Hippolyta   I was with Hercules and Cadmus once,
When in a wood of Crete they bayed the bear
With hounds of Sparta: never did I hear
Such gallant chiding, for besides the groves,
The skies, the fountains, every region near
Seemed all one mutual cry. I never heard
So musical a discord, such sweet thunder.

Theseus   My hounds are bred out of the Spartan kind:
So flewed, so sanded; and their heads are hung
With ears that sweep away the morning dew –   120
Crook-kneed, and dewlapped like Thessalian bulls;
Slow in pursuit; but matched in mouth like bells,
Each under each. A cry more tuneable
Was never hollaed to, nor cheered with horn,
In Crete, in Sparta, nor in Thessaly.
Judge when you hear. But, soft, what nymphs are these?

Egeus   My lord, this is my daughter here asleep –
And this Lysander – this Demetrius is –
This Helena, old Nedar's Helena.
I wonder of their being here together.   130

Theseus   No doubt they rose up early to observe
The rite of May; and, hearing our intent,
Came here in grace of our solemnity.
But, speak, Egeus, is not this the day
That Hermia should give answer of her choice?

Egeus   It is, my lord.

Theseus   Go, bid the huntsmen wake them with their horns.

---

103 **observation:** to a morn of May. See Act I/*Scene 1*/line 167
104 **vaward:** forepart (since it is early)
106 **Uncouple:** release
114 **chiding:** barking
119 **flewed:** with hanging chops
     sanded: of sandy colour

DEMETRIUS.
WEDDING.
BEN CAMPBELL

A MIDSUMMER NIGHTS DREAM. STRATFORD ONT.

Horns sound; the lovers awake with a start

	Good morrow, friends. Saint Valentine is past;	
	Begin these wood-birds but to couple now?	
Lysander	Pardon, my lord.	
Theseus	I pray you all, stand up.	140
	I know you two are rival enemies.	
	How comes this gentle concord in the world,	
	That hatred is far from jealousy,	
	To sleep by hate, and fear no enmity?	
Lysander	My lord, I shall reply amazedly,	
	Half sleep, half waking. But as yet, I swear,	
	I cannot truly say how I came here.	
	But, as I think – for truly would I speak,	
	And now I do bethink me, so it is:	
	I came with Hermia hither. Our intent	150
	Was to be gone from Athens where we might,	
	Without the peril of the Athenian law –	
Egeus	Enough, enough, my lord; you have enough.	
	I beg the law, the law, upon his head.	
	They would have stol'n away, they would, Demetrius,	
	Thereby to have defeated you and me:	
	You of your wife, and me of my consent;	
	Of my consent that she should be your wife.	
Demetrius	My lord, fair Helen told me of their stealth	
	Of this their purpose hither to this wood,	160
	And I in fury hither followed them;	
	Fair Helena in fancy following me.	
	But, my good lord, I wot not by what power –	
	But by some power it is – my love to Hermia,	
	Melted as the snow, seems to me now	
	As the remembrance of an idle gaud	
	Which in my childhood I did dote upon:	
	And all the faith, the virtue of my heart,	
	The object and the pleasure of mine eye,	
	Is only Helena. To her, my lord,	170
	Was I betrothed ere I saw Hermia:	
	But, like in sickness, did I loathe this food,	
	But, as in health, come to my natural taste,	
	Now I do wish it, love it, long for it,	
	And will for evermore be true to it.	
Theseus	Fair lovers, you are fortunately met.	[176]
	Of this discourse we more will hear anon.	
	Egeus, I will overbear your will;	
	For in the temple, by and by, with us,	

143 **jealousy:** suspicion

Theseus and Hippolyta.
Theseus: "Fair lovers, you are fortunately met."

	These couples shall eternally be knit.	180
	And, for the morning now is something worn,	
	Our purposed hunting shall be set aside.	
	Away with us, to Athens! Three and three,	
	We'll hold a feast in great solemnity.	
	Come, Hippolyta.	

Exeunt Theseus, Hippolyta, Egeus, and their train

Demetrius These things seem small and undistinguishable,
Like far-off mountains turnéd into clouds.

Hermia Methinks I see these things with parted eye,
When everything seems double.

Helena So methinks:
And I have found Demetrius like a jewel, 190
Mine own, and not mine own.

Demetrius Are you sure
That we are awake? It seems to me,
That yet we sleep, we dream. Do not you think
The duke was here, and bid us follow him?

Hermia Yea, and my father.

Helena And Hippolyta.

Lysander And he did bid us to follow to the temple.

Demetrius Why then, we are awake; let's follow him,
And by the way let us recount our dreams.

Exeunt [Scene 23]

Bottom *(awaking)* When my cue comes, call me, and I
will answer. My next is, 'Most fair Pyramus.' Heigh- 200
ho. *(He looks about him.)* Peter Quince!
Flute, the bellows-mender! Snout, the tinker! Starveling!
God's my life! Stol'n hence, and left me asleep! I have
had a most rare vision. I have had a dream – past the
wit of man to say what dream it was. Man is but an
ass, if he go about to expound this dream. *(He rises.)*
Methought I was – there is no man can tell what.
(He passes his hand across his head, touching his ears.)
Methought I was, and methought I had – but man is but a
patched fool, if he will offer to say what methought I 210
had. The eye of man hath not heard, the ear of man
hath not seen, man's hand is not able to taste, his tongue
to conceive, nor his heart to report, what my dream was.
I will get Peter Quince to write a ballad of this dream:
it shall be called Bottom's Dream; because it hath no
bottom: and I will sing it in the latter end of our play,
before the duke. Peradventure, to make it the more
gracious, I shall sing it at her death. *Exit*

---

180 **knit:** married   215-6 **hath no bottom:** is unfathomable

Bottom to Snout, Snug, Starveling, and Flute:
   "Masters, I am to discourse wonders: but ask
   me not what; for if I tell you, I am not true Athenian.
   I will tell you every thing, right as it fell out."

Scene 2

The room in Peter Quince's cottage

Enter Quince, Flute, Snout, and Starveling

Quince	Have you sent to Bottom's house? Is he come home yet?
Starveling	He cannot be heard of. Out of doubt he is transported.
Flute	If he come not then the play is marred. It goes not forward, doth it?
Quince	It is not possible. You have not a man in all Athens able to discharge Pyramus but he.
Flute	No, he hath simply the best wit of any handicraft man in Athens.
Quince	Yea, and the best person too – and he is a very paramour for a sweet voice.
Flute	You must say 'paragon.' A paramour is – God bless us – a thing of naught.

Enter Snug

Snug	Masters, the duke is coming from the temple, and there is two or three lords and ladies more married – if our sport had gone forward, we had all been made men.
Flute	O sweet bully Bottom! Thus hath he lost sixpence a day during his life: he could not have 'scaped sixpence a day. An the duke had not given him sixpence a day for playing Pyramus, I'll be hanged. He would have deserved it. Sixpence a day in Pyramus, or nothing.

Enter Bottom

Bottom	Where are these lads? Where are these hearts?
Quince	Bottom! O most courageous day! O most happy hour!

They all crowd about him

Bottom	Masters, I am to discourse wonders: but ask me not what; for if I tell you, I am not true Athenian. I will tell you every thing, right as it fell out.
Quince	Let us hear, sweet Bottom.

10

20

[23]

---

4 **transported:** carried away by fairies
5 **marred:** hindered
8 **discharge:** perform
9 **wit:** intellect
12 **paramour:** illicit partner
17 **made men:** made our fortunes

Bottom　　　Not a word of me. All that I will tell you is, that the　　30
duke hath dined. Get your apparel together – good
strings to your beards, new ribbons to your pumps –
meet presently at the palace, every man look o'er his
part – for the short and the long is, our play is preferred.
In any case, let Thisbe have clean linen; and let not
him that plays the lion pare his nails; for they shall hang
out for the lion's claws. And, most dear actors, eat no
onions, nor garlic; for we are to utter sweet breath; and
I do not doubt but to hear them say, it is a sweet comedy.
No more words. Away, go away!　　40
Exeunt

---

34 **preferred**: recommended

Act Fifth

Scene 1 [Scene 24]

The hall in the palace of Duke Theseus

Enter Theseus and Hippolyta followed by Philostrate, lords, and attendants [0]

Hippolyta 'Tis strange, my Theseus, that these lovers speak of.
Theseus More strange than true. I never may believe
These antique fables, nor these fairy toys.
Lovers and madmen have such seething brains,
Such shaping fantasies, that apprehend
More than cool reason ever comprehends.
The lunatic, the lover, and the poet
Are of imagination all compact.
One sees more devils than vast hell can hold;
That is, the madman. The lover, all as frantic. 10
Sees Helen's beauty in a brow of Egypt.
The poet's eye, in a fine frenzy rolling,
Doth glance from heaven to earth,
  from earth to heaven;
And as imagination bodies forth
The forms of things unknown, the poet's pen
Turns them to shapes, and gives to airy nothing
A local habitation and a name.
Such tricks hath strong imagination,
That, if it would apprehend some joy,
It comprehends some bringer of that joy; 20
Or in the night, imagining some fear,
How easy is a bush supposed a bear!

---

3 **antique:** ancient, or antic
  toys: tales
5 **apprehend:** conceive, imagine
6 **comprehends:** understands

Theseus to Hippolyta:
"What revels are in hand? Is there no play,
To ease the anguish of a torturing hour?"

Hippolyta	But all the story of the night told over,
	And all their minds transfigured so together,
	More witnesseth than fancy's images,
	And grows to something of great constancy.
	But, howsoever, strange and admirable.
Theseus	Here comes the lovers, full of joy and mirth.

Enter Lysander and Hermia, Demetrius and Helena

	Joy, gentle friends! Joy and fresh days of love	
	Accompany your hearts!	
Lysander	More than to us	30
	Wait in your royal walks, your board, your bed!	
Theseus	Come now; what masques, what dances shall we have,	
	To wear away this long age of three hours	
	Between our after-supper and bed-time?	
	Where is our usual manager of mirth?	
	What revels are in hand? Is there no play,	[36-37]
	To ease the anguish of a torturing hour?	
	Call Philostrate.	
Philostrate	Here, mighty Theseus.	
Theseus	Say, what abridgment have you for this evening?	
	What masque? What music? How shall we beguile	40
	The lazy time, if not with some delight?	
Philostrate	There is a brief how many sports are ripe.	
	Make a choice of which your highness will see first.	
Theseus	'The Battle with the Centaurs, to be sung,	
	By an Athenian eunuch to the harp.'	
	We'll none of that. That have I told my love,	[46-47]
	In glory of my kinsman Hercules.	
	'The riot of the tipsy Bacchanals,	
	Tearing the Thracian singer in their rage.'	
	That is an old device; and it was played	[50-51]
	When I from Thebes came last a conqueror.	
	'The thrice three Muses mourning for the death	
	Of learning, late deceased in beggary.'	
	That is some satire, keen and critical,	
	Not sorting with a nuptial ceremony.	
	'A tedious brief scene of young Pyramus	
	And his love Thisbe; very tragical mirth.'	
	Merry and tragical! Tedious and brief!	
	That is, hot ice and wondrous strange snow.	
	How shall we find the concord of this discord?	60

25 **More witnesseth:** gives more evidence
34 **after-supper:** dessert banquet
42 **brief:** list, summary
49 **Thracian singer:** Orpheus

Philostrate	A play there is, my lord, some ten words long;
	Which is as brief as I have known a play;
	But by ten words, my lord, it is too long;
	Which makes it tedious: for in all the play
	There is not one word apt, one player fitted.
	And tragical, my noble lord, it is;
	For Pyramus therein doth kill himself.
	Which when I saw rehearsed, I must confess,
	Made mine eyes water; but more merry tears
	The passion of loud laughter never shed.	70
Theseus	What are they that do play it?
Philostrate	Hard-handed men, that work in Athens here,
	Which never laboured in their minds till now;
	And now have toiled their unbreathed memories
	With this same play, against your nuptial.
Theseus	And we will hear it.
Philostrate	No, my noble lord,
	It is not for you: I have heard it over,
	And it is nothing, nothing in the world;
	Unless you can find sport in their intents,
	Extremely stretched and conned with cruel pain,	80
	To do you service.
Theseus	I will hear that play:
	For never anything can be amiss,
	When simpleness and duty tender it.
	Go, bring them in – and take your places, ladies.

Exit Philostrate

Hippolyta	I love not to see wretchedness o'ercharged,
	And duty in his service perishing.
Theseus	Why, gentle sweet, you shall see no such thing.
Hippolyta	He says they can do nothing in this kind.
Theseus	The kinder we, to give them thanks for nothing.
	Our sport shall be to take what they mistake:	90
	And what poor duty cannot do, noble respect
	Takes it in might, not merit.
	Where I have come, great clerks have purposéd
	To greet me with premediated welcomes;
	Where I have seen them shiver and look pale,	[95]
	Make periods in the midst of sentences,

---

74 **unbreathed:** unexercised, unused
75 **against:** in preparation for
83 **simpleness:** innocence
85 **wretchedness:** lower classes
91 **respect:** consideration
92 **in might, not merit:** takes the will for the deed

Throttle their practised accent in their fears,
And in conclusion dumbly have broke off,
Not paying me a welcome. Trust me, sweet,
Out of this silence yet I picked a welcome;   100
And in the modesty of fearful duty
I read as much as from the rattling tongue
Of saucy and audacious eloquence.
Love, therefore, and tongue-tied simplicity
In least speak most, to my capacity.

Re-enter Philostrate

Philostrate   So please your grace, the Prologue is addressed.
Theseus   Let him approach.

Enter Quince   [Scene 25]

Quince   'If we offend, it is with our good will.
    That you should think, we come not to offend,
But with good will. To show our simple skill,   110
    That is the true beginning of our end.
Consider then, we come but in despite.
    We do not come, as minding to content you,
Our true intent is. All for your delight,
    We are not here. That you should here repent you,
The actors are at hand: and by their show,
You shall know all, that you are like to know.'   *Exit*
Theseus   This fellow doth not stand upon points.
Lysander   He hath rid his prologue like a rough colt:
He knows not the stop. A good moral, my lord –   [120-21]
it is not enough to speak; but to speak true.
Hippolyta   Indeed he hath played on his prologue like a child
on a recorder — a sound, but not in government.
Theseus   His speech was like a tangled chain; nothing   [124-25]
impaired, but all disordered. Who is next?

Enter Pyramus and Thisbe, Wall, Moonshine, and Lion,
as in dumb-show, with Quince for the Presenter

Quince   'Gentles, perchance you wonder at this show,
    But wonder on, till truth make all things plain.
This man is Pyramus, if you would know:

---

104 **simplicity:** sincerity
105 **to my capacity:** in my opinion
116 **show:** mime-show
123 **government:** control

	This beauteous lady Thisbe is, certain.	
	This man, with lime and rough-cast, doth present	130

This beauteous lady Thisbe is, certain.
This man, with lime and rough-cast, doth present   130
    Wall, that vile Wall which did these lovers sunder:
And through Wall's chink, poor souls, they are content
    To whisper. At the which let no man wonder.
This man, with lantern, dog, and bush of thorn,
    Presenteth Moonshine. For, if you will know,
By moonshine did these lovers think no scorn
    To meet at Ninus' tomb, there, there to woo:
This grisly beast – which Lion hight by name –
The trusty Thisbe, coming first by night,
Did scare away, or rather did affright: 140
And, as she fled, her mantle she did fall:
    Which Lion vile with bloody mouth did stain.
Anon comes Pyramus, sweet youth, and tall,
    And finds his trusty Thisbe's mantle slain:
Whereat, with blade, with bloody blameful blade,
    He bravely broached his boiling bloody breast.
And Thisbe, tarrying in mulberry shade,
    His dagger drew, and died. For all the rest,
Let Lion, Moonshine, Wall, and lovers twain,
At large discourse, while here they do remain.'   150

Theseus   I wonder if the lion be to speak.

Demetrius   No wonder, my lord – one lion may,
    when many asses do.   *Exeunt all save Wall and Pyramus*

Wall   'In this same interlude it doth befall
    That I, one Snout by name, present a wall: [155]
    And such a wall, as I would have you think,
    That had in it a crannied hole or chink:
    Through which the lovers, Pyramus and Thisbe,
    Did whisper often very secretly.
    This loam, this rough-cast, and this stone doth show   160
    That I am that same wall; the truth is so.
    And this the cranny is, right and sinister,
    Through which the fearful lovers are to whisper.'   [163]

Theseus   Would you desire lime and hair to speak better?

Demetrius   It is the wittiest partition that ever I heard
    discourse, my lord.

Theseus   Pyramus draws near the wall: silence!

Pyramus   'O grim-looked night! O night with hue so black!
    O night, which ever art when day is not: 170
    O night, O night, alack, alack, alack,
    I fear my Thisbe's promise is forgot.
    And thou, O wall! O sweet, O lovely wall!
    That stand'st between her father's ground and mine,

Thou wall, O wall! O sweet and lovely wall!
  Show me thy chink to blink through with mine eyne.
Thanks, courteous wall. Jove shield thee well for this!
  But what see I? No Thisbe do I see.
O wicked wall, through whom I see no bliss,
  Cursed be thy stones for thus deceiving me!'   180

Theseus The wall, methinks, being sensible, should
curse again.

Pyramus No, in truth, sir, he should not. 'Deceiving
me' is Thisbe's cue: she is to enter now, and I am to spy
her through the wall. You shall see, it will fall pat
as I told you. Yonder she comes.

Enter Thisbe

Thisbe 'O wall! Full often hast thou heard my moans,
  For parting my fair Pyramus and me.
My cherry lips have often kissed thy stones;
  Thy stones with lime and hair knit up in thee.'   190

Pyramus 'I see a voice: now will I to the chink,
  To spy an I can hear my Thisbe's face. Thisbe!'

Thisbe 'My love! thou art my love, I think.'

Pyramus 'Think what thou wilt, I am thy lover's grace;
  And, like Limander, am I trusty still.'   [195-98]

Thisbe 'And I like Helen, till the Fates me kill.'

Pyramus 'Not Shafalus to Procrus was so true.'

Thisbe 'As Shafalus to Procrus, I to you.'

Pyramus 'O! kiss me through the hole of this vile wall.'

Thisbe 'I kiss the wall's hole; not your lips at all.'   200

Pyramus 'Wilt thou at Ninny's tomb meet me
straightway?'

Thisbe ''Tide life, 'tide death, I come without delay.'

                      Exeunt Pyramus and Thisbe

Wall 'Thus have I, Wall, my part dischargéd so;
  And being done, thus Wall away doth go.'   *Exit Wall*

Theseus Now is the mural down between the two
neighbours.

Demetrius No remedy, my lord, when walls are so
wilful to hear without warning.

Hippolyta This is the silliest stuff that ever I heard.

Theseus The best in this kind are but shadows: and   210
the worst are no worse, if imagination amend them.

Hippolyta It must be your imagination then; and not
theirs.

Theseus If we imagine no worse of them than they of
themselves, they may pass for excellent men.
Here come two noble beasts in, a man and a lion.

Thisbe, Pyramus, and Wall.
Pyramus: " 'O! kiss me through the hole of this vile wall.' "
Thisbe: " 'I kiss the wall's hole; not your lips at all.' "

Enter Lion and Moonshine

Lion	'You ladies, you, whose gentle hearts do fear
	The smallest monstrous mouse that creeps on floor,
	May now perchance both quake and tremble here,
	When lion rough in wildest rage doth roar.
	Then know that I, as Snug the joiner am
	A lion fell, nor else no lion's dam.
	For if I should as lion come in strife
	Into this place, 'twere pity on my life.'
Theseus	A very gentle beast, and of a good
	conscience.
Demetrius	The very best at a beast, my lord, that
	e'er I saw.
Lysander	This lion is a very fox for his valour.
Theseus	True: and a goose for his discretion.
Demetrius	Not so, my lord, for his valour cannot
	carry his discretion; and the fox carries the goose.
Theseus	His discretion, I am sure, cannot carry his valour,
	for the goose carries not the fox. It is well: leave
	it to his discretion, and let us listen to the moon.
Moonshine	'This lanthorn doth the hornéd moon present' –
Demetrius	He should have worn the horns on his head.
Theseus	He is no crescent, and his horns are
	invisible within the circumference.
Moonshine	'This lanthorn doth the hornéd moon present,
	Myself the man i' th' moon do seem to be.'
Theseus	This is the greatest error of all the rest: the
	man should be put into the lantern. How is it
	else the man i' th' moon?
Demetrius	He dares not come there for the candle –
	for, you see, it is already in snuff.
Hippolyta	I am aweary of this moon. Would he
	would change!
Theseus	It appears, by his small light of discretion,
	that he is in the wane: but yet, in courtesy, in
	all reason, we must stay the time.
Lysander	Proceed, Moon.
Moonshine	All that I have to say, is, to tell you that
	the lanthorn is the moon, I the man i' th' moon,
	this thorn-bush my thorn-bush, and this dog my dog.

220

230
[231-34]

240

250

---

222 **fell:** fierce (or, a skin)
236 **lanthorn:** pronounced lant-horn (lantern)
237 **on his head:** as a cuckold
245 **for the candle:** for fear of the candle
246 **in snuff:** in a passion; in need of snuffing

Demetrius	Why, all these should be in the lantern; for all these are in the moon. But, silence; here comes Thisbe.

Enter Thisbe

Thisbe	'This is old Ninny's tomb. Where is my love?'	
Lion	*(roars)* 'Oh' –	250

Exit Thisbe, pursued by Lion

Demetrius	Well roared, Lion.	
Theseus	Well run, Thisbe.	
Hippolyta	Well shone, Moon. Truly, the moon shines with a good grace.	*Lion paws Thisbe's mantle*
Theseus	Well moused, Lion.	
Demetrius	And then came Pyramus.	

Enter Pyramus; exit Lion

Lysander	And so the lion vanished.	
Pyramus	'Sweet moon, I thank thee for thy sunny beams.	
	I thank thee, moon, for shining now so bright.	
	For, by thy gracious, golden, glittering gleams,	260
	I trust to take of truest Thisbe sight.	
	But stay . . . O spite!	
	But mark, poor knight,	
	What dreadful dole is here!	
	Eyes, do you see?	
	How can it be?	
	O dainty duck, O dear!	
	Thy mantle good,	
	What, stained with blood?	
	Approach, ye Furies fell!	270
	O Fates, come, come,	
	Cut thread and thrum,	
	Quail, crush, conclude, and quell!'	
Theseus	This passion – and the death of a dear friend – would go near to make a man look sad.	
Hippolyta	Beshrew my heart, but I pity the man.	
Pyramus	'O wherefore, Nature, didst thou lions frame?	
	Since lion vile hath here deflowered my dear.	
	Which is – no, no – which was the fairest dame,	
	That lived, that loved, that liked, that looked, with cheer.	290
	Come, tears, confound,	
	Out, sword, and wound	
	The pap of Pyramus:	
	Ay, that left pap,	

Lysander, Pyramus, Thisbe, and Quince.
Thisbe: "'Asleep, my love?
  What, dead, my dove?
  O Pyramus, arise,
  Speak, speak. Quite dumb?
  Dead, dead . . .'"

	Where heart doth hop.	*He stabs himself*
	Thus die I, thus, thus, thus.	
	Now am I dead,	
	Now am I fled,	
	My soul is in the sky.	
	Tongue, lose thy light!	300
	Moon, take thy flight!	*Exit Moonshine*
	Now die, die, die, die, die.'	*He muffles his face*

Demetrius No die, but an ace, for him – for he is but one. [303-07]

Lysander Less than an ace, man – for he is dead,
he is nothing.

Theseus With the help of a surgeon, he might yet
recover, and prove an ass.

Hippolyta How chance Moonshine is gone before
Thisbe comes back and finds her lover?

Theseus She will find him by starlight. Here she 310
comes, and her passion ends the play.

Enter Thisbe

Hippolyta Methinks she should not use a long one [312-16]
for such a Pyramus: I hope she will be brief.

Demetrius A mote will turn the balance, which
Pyramus, which Thisbe, is the better: he for a man,
God warr'nt us; she for a woman, God bless us.

Lysander She hath spied him already with those sweet eyes.

Thisbe discovers Pyramus

Demetrius And thus she means, *videlicet*. [318]

Thisbe

  'Asleep, my love?
  What, dead, my dove? 320
O Pyramus, arise,
  Speak, speak. Quite dumb?
  Dead, dead. A tomb
Must cover thy sweet eyes.
  These lily lips,
  This cherry nose,
These yellow cowslip cheeks,
  Are gone, are gone:
  Lovers, make moan:
His eyes were green as leeks. 330
  O Sisters Three, [331]
  Come, come, to me,

---

314 **mote:** moth
318 **videlicet:** you may see

With hands as pale as milk,
    Lay them in gore,
    Since you have shore
With shears his thread of silk.
    Tongue, not a word:
    Come, trusty sword,
Come, blade, my breast imbrue.   *Stabs herself*
    And farewell, friends: 340
    Thus Thisbe ends:
Adieu, adieu, adieu.'   *She dies*

Enter Lion, Moonshine, and Wall

Theseus   Moonshine and Lion are left to bury the dead.
Demetrius Ay, and Wall too.
Lion   No, I assure you, the wall is down that parted
            their fathers. *(He plucks a paper from his bosom.)*
            Will it please you to see the Epilogue, or hear a
            Bergomask dance between two of our company?
Theseus   No Epilogue, I pray you – for your play needs
            no excuse. Never excuse; for when the players are all   350
            dead, there need none to be blamed. . . . Marry, if he that
            writ it had played Pyramus and hanged himself in
            Thisbe's garter, it would have been a fine tragedy: and
            so it is truly, and very notably discharged. . . . But come,
            your Bergomask: let your Epilogue alone.   [355]
                                  A dance. Exeunt Bottom and his fellows

The iron tongue of midnight hath told twelve!
Lovers, to bed – 'tis almost fairy time.
I fear we shall out-sleep the coming morn,
As much as we this night have overwatched.
This palpable-gross play hath well beguiled   360
The heavy gait of night. Sweet friends, to bed.
A fortnight hold we this solemnity,
In nightly revels, and new jollity.   *Exeunt*

Enter Puck, broom in hand   [Scene 26]

Puck   Now the hungry lion roars,
        And the wolf behowls the moon;
      Whilst the heavy ploughman snores,
        All with weary task fordone.

---

339 **imbrue:** stain with blood (pierce)   360 **palpable-gross:** obviously crude
356 **told:** counted (chimed)   365 **behowls:** howls at
359 **overwatched:** stayed awake   367 **fordone:** exhausted
      longer than normal

Now the wasted brands do glow,
   Whilst the screech-owl, screeching loud,
Puts the wretch that lies in woe   370
   In remembrance of a shroud.
Now it is the time of night,
   That the graves, all gaping wide,
Every one lets forth his sprite,
   In the church-way paths to glide.
And we fairies, that do run
   By the triple Hecate's team,   [377]
From the presence of the sun,
   Following darkness like a dream,
Now are frolic: not a mouse   380
   Shall disturb this hallowed house.
I am sent with broom before,
   To sweep the dust behind the door.

Enter Oberon, Titania, and their train

Oberon   Through the house give glimmering light,
   By the dead and drowsy fire,
Every elf and fairy sprite
   Hop as light as bird from briar,
And this ditty after me
Sing, and dance it trippingly.
Titania   First rehearse your song by rote,   390
To each word a warbling note.
Hand in hand, with fairy grace,
Will we sing and bless this place.   *Song and dance* [393]

SONG
Now, until the break of day,
Through this house each fairy stray.
To the best bride-bed will we:
Which by us shall blessèd be:
And the issue, there create,
Ever shall be fortunate:
So shall all the couples three   400
Ever true in loving be:
And the blots of Nature's hand
Shall not in their issue stand.
Never mole, hare-lip, nor scar,
Nor mark prodigious, such as are

---

368 **wasted brands:** burned-down logs
398 **issue:** children

Oberon to his train:
"Every elf and fairy sprite
  Hop as light as bird from briar,
And sing this ditty after me..."

Despiséd in nativity,
Shall upon their children be.
With this field-dew consecrate,
Each fairy take his gait,
And each several chamber bless, 410
Through this palace, with sweet peace,
And the owner of it blest,
Ever shall in safety rest.
    Trip away:
    Make no stay:
Meet me all by break of day.

Epilogue

Puck   If we shadows have offended,
Think but this, and all is mended,
That you have but slumbred here,
While these visions did appear. 420
And this weak and idle theme,
No more yielding but a dream,
Gentles, do not reprehend.
If you pardon, we will mend.
And, as I am an honest Puck,
If we have unearnéd luck
Now to 'scape the serpent's tongue,
We will make amends, ere long:
Else the Puck a liar call.
So, good night unto you all. 430
Give me your hands, if we be friends:
And Robin shall restore amends. *Exit*

Puck: "So, good night unto you all."

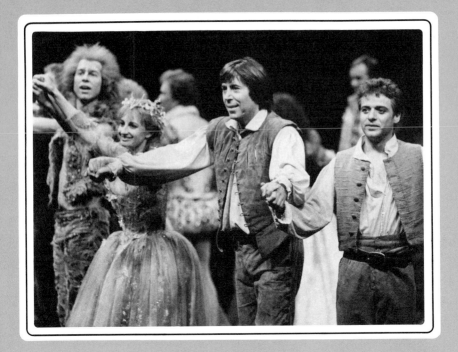

Puck, Titania, Bottom, and Flute join hands with the rest of the cast
for a curtain call.

Stratford Festival Edition Emendations

In the 1984 Stratford Festival Production of *A Midsummer Night's Dream*, the following changes were made in the text for various reasons. Occasionally a new word was interjected in order to complement the action of a scene, or an obscure word was changed to a more accessible equivalent. In both cases, anachronism was avoided by using a word that would have been in use in Shakespeare's time.

Often entire lines were cut. Although their meaning was clear to the actor or to someone reading the words on the page with the aid of a glossary, it was found that certain opaque references interfered with the action of the play.

Although such liberties may startle the purist, they ultimately lead to a greater enjoyment of the play on the part of the general audience.

Act I / Scene 1

line 0:   A prologue preceded the play, in which Theseus's army defeated Hippolyta's. This battle is referred to in the first scene of the play.

line 143:   *momentany* was changed to *momentary*.

lines 173-174: "And by the Fire . . . was seen." Dido, Queen of Carthage, burned herself on a funeral pyre when the Trojan Aeneas, her lover, sailed away. Marlow and Nashe wrote a play on the subject, probably a few years earlier than Shakespeare wrote *Midsummer Night's Dream*.

Act I / Scene 2

line 11:   "the most lamentable comedy" parodies an actual play published in 1570 entitled "A lamentable tragedy mixed full of pleasant mirth, containing the life of Cambyses, King of Persia."

line 90:   After Quince said "barefaced," Snug roared like a lion.

Patricia Conolly as Hippolyta. ". . . the moon, like a silver bow
New bent in heaven, shall behold the night
Of our solemnities." (Act I/Scene 1, lines 9–11)

Act II / *Scene 1*

line 7:
"moones sphere." It was believed by the astronomers of Shakespeare's day that the moon was fixed in a hollow crystalline sphere that revolved around the earth every twenty-four hours.

line 23:
"changling." A changling was a child left by fairies in exchange for a stolen one, but in this case, it is the stolen child.

line 54:
" 'tailor' cries." The meaning of this is not clear, but Johnson wrote: "The custom of crying "tailor" at a sudden fall backwards I think I remember to have observed. He that slips beside his chair falls as a tailor squats upon his board."

lines 81-117:
"These are the forgeries . . . and original." This speech is arguably a topical reference to a particularly bad summer in 1594. It presents a strong poetic image of confusion in the world of nature. See "Observations on a *Midsummer Night's Dream*," page 00.

line 101:
"cheer" is a commonly accepted emendation for the earlier "here." "Cheer" would anticipate the following line.

line 158:
"fair Vestal" one may assume refers to Queen Elizabeth I.

line 231:
"Apollo flies . . . the chase." Daphne fled from Apollo and was changed into a laurel tree in order to escape him.

line 266:
After "her love," Puck delivered his line (268), then Oberon ended the scene with line 267.

Act II / *Scene 2*

lines 17-20:
"Never harm . . . with lullaby." These lines were cut.

lines 25-28:
"Philomel . . . lulla, lullaby." These lines were cut.

line 112:
"Nature shows art" is the commonly accepted modern emendation for the earlier "Nature shows her art."

Act III / *Scene 1*

line 22:
"eight and six" means lines of eight and six syllables, a metre common in ballads.

lines 53-54:
"bush of thorns" was commonly attributed to the man in the moon.

line 77:	Bottom questioned Quince's correction and said: "Odorous savours sweet?" He then continued the speech as if ignoring the correction.
line 90:	"Ninny" is a fool. In Ovid's story of Pyramus and Thisbe, they met at Ninus's tomb. Ninus was the mythical founder of Nineveh.
line 136:	After "friends," Bottom delivered his first "hee-haw."
line 151:	Each fairy responded with his line as soon as Titania said his name.
line 173:	*gentleman* was changed to *maiden.*
line 177:	*Master* was changed to *Mistress.*
line 187:	"The moon . . . wat'ry eye." It was thought that dew originated in the moon.
line 189:	After "chastity," Bottom responded with "hee-haw."

Act III / Scene 2

line 404:	After Puck says "to plainer ground," Lysander said: "Demetrius."

Act IV / Scene 1

line 29:	"the tongs and the bones" were simple musical instruments. The tongs were struck by a piece of metal and the bones were two flat pieces of bone held between the fingers and rattled against each other.
line 35:	"fetch thee new nuts" was emended to "fetch thee thence new nuts" in order to correct the metre.
line 41:	The keen observer will note that "woodbine" means "honeysuckle" in another of Shakespeare's comedies, *Much Ado About Nothing.* Here it seems to mean "bindweed," which can grow entangled with honeysuckle.
line 84:	"Sound, music." was transposed to line 85, to follow "these sleepers be." The following lyrics were used in a song accompanying the dance: All yee woods and trees and bowers All yee virtues and yee powers Yee that dwell in all the lakes

In the pleasant springs and brakes
Move your feet to our sound
Whilst we greet all the grove
Ever holy ever young
Ever honoured ever young
Move your feet to our sound
Whilst we greet all this ground
Move your feet to our sound
Whilst we greet all this ground.

line 176:   "Fair lovers ... met." This line was cut so that Theseus could respond immediately to the information given in Demetrius's speech.

Act IV | *Scene 2*

line 23:   After "Where are these lads?" Quince said: "Bottom," which was transposed from line 24.

Act V | *Scene 1*

line 0:   Egeus was included in the party.

lines 36-37:   "What revels ... torturing hour?" These lines were cut to expedite the action of the scene.

lines 46-47:   "That have I ... Hercules." These lines were cut.

lines 50-51:   "and it was played ... a conqueror." These lines were cut.

line 95:   *Where* was changed to *When*.

lines 120-121:   "A good moral ... speak true." These lines were cut to expedite the action of the scene.

lines 124-125:   "His speech ... all disordered." These lines were cut.

line 155:   After "a wall," Quince interjected: "Louder."

line 163:   "whisper" was changed to "whinisper," in order to rhyme with "sinister" in the preceding line. Quince then corrected him. Wall has stretched out his hand and formed a circle with his thumb and finger.

lines 195-198:   "Limander" is possibly a corruption of Alexander, which was another name for Paris, lover of Helen of Troy. "Shafalus and Procrus" is a corruption of "Cephalus and Procris," legendary lovers whose story is told in Ovid's *Metamorphoses*.

lines 231-234: "Not so ... discretion, and." These lines were cut to expedite the action of the play.

lines 303-307: "No die ... prove an ass." These lines were cut to expedite the action of the play. "Die" was one of a pair of dice and "ace" was a single spot on the die. "Ace" is close in pronunciation to "ass," providing the pun in line 307.

lines 312-316: "Methinks ... God bless us." These lines were cut.

line 318: "And thus ... *videlicet*." This line was cut.

line 331: "Sisters Three" are the Fates.

line 355: The "mechanicals" performed their Bergomask, which is a rustic dance after the manner of Bergamo, in Italy. The dance was accompanied by the following song:

> Trip and go, heave and ho
> Up and down, to and fro
> From the town to the grove
> Two by two, let us rove
> A maying, a playing
> Love hath no ho ho
> gainsaying
> So, merrily trip
> So, merrily trip
> So, merrily trip and go.
>
> So merrily trip and, an
> So, merrily trip
> And go, and go, and go.

line 377: The goddess Hecate ruled as Luna and Cynthia in heaven; as Diana on earth; as Proserpine and Hecate in hell. Here Puck refers to her as goddess of the moon and night.

line 393: The "song and dance" of the stage direction was performed with the following lyrics:

> Bless this house with joy and gladness
> Gentle love and human kindness
> Fields and forests grace them safely
> Fish and fawn watch them daily.
>
> Night owls guard the peaceful sleep
> Larks and swallows bring them cheer
> Bless their children with peace and plenty
> May they live ever loved and loving.
>
> La, la, la, la,
> La, la, la, la,
> La, la, la, la,
> La, la, la, la.

STARVELING.
EDWARD ATIENZA.

MIDSUMMER NIGHTS DREAM   STRATFORD ONTARIO.

Biographical Notes

John Hirsch

Artistic Director John Hirsch directed *As You Like It* and *Tartuffe* for the 1983 Stratford Festival season. His other Stratford credits include *The Tempest* and *Mary Stuart*, 1982; *The Three Sisters*, 1976; *Hamlet* and *Satyricon*, 1969; *A Midsummer Night's Dream* and *The Three Musketeers*, 1968; *Richard III* and *Colours in the Dark*, 1967; *Henry VI*, 1966; and *The Cherry Orchard*, 1965.

Mr. Hirsch emigrated from Hungary to Canada in 1947. After graduating from the University of Manitoba he co-founded the Manitoba Theatre Centre and Winnipeg's Rainbow Stage. Former Consulting Artistic Director of the Seattle Repertory Theatre, he has staged productions at major theatres in North America, including the Guthrie Theater in Minneapolis.

He has won the Outer Circle Critics' Award for *St. Joan* at the Lincoln Center Repertory Theater, New York; an Obie Award for *AC-DC* at Brooklyn's Chelsea Theatre; and the Los Angeles Drama Critics' Award for *The Dybbuk* at the Mark Taper Forum, a work he also translated and adapted, and which brought him the Canadian Authors' Association Literary Award. His latest production at the Mark Taper was *Number Our Days*. He has also directed Verdi's *The Masked Ball* at the New York City Opera and Joseph Heller's *We Bombed in New Haven* on Broadway.

As former head of CBC Television Drama, Mr. Hirsch developed many outstanding drama projects, among them *A Gift to Last*, for which he received the Prix Anik Award; *For The Record*; *King of Kensington*; and *Sarah*, starring Zoe Caldwell, which was nominated for an International Emmy Award.

Mr. Hirsch is a member of the Order of Canada.

Desmond Heeley

In 1983 Desmond Heeley created designs for *As You Like It* and *The Country Wife*, which marked his 25th production for the Stratford Festival since 1957. He also designed the stage itself for the Third Stage. During his illustrious career Mr. Heeley has worked for most major theatre, opera, and ballet companies throughout Europe, Canada, and the United States, and won two Tony Awards for the Broadway production of *Rosencrantz and Guildenstern* in 1967. His most memorable Festival productions include *Arms and the Man*, 1982; *Coriolanus*, 1981; *Titus Andronicus*, 1978-80; *She Stoops to Conquer*, 1972-73; *The Duchess of Malfi*, 1971; *Cyrano*, 1962; and *Hamlet*, 1957.

His most current work includes Lance Mulcahy's *Sweet Will* in Toronto, a "marvellous" musical cabaret of Shakespeare's songs; and a new production of *La Sylphide* for Eric Bruhn, Baryshnikov, and the American Ballet Theatre, which opened in New York in June, 1983.

Elliott Hayes

Elliott Hayes is the Associate Literary Manager of the Stratford Festival. For the 1982 Festival Season he was assistant director of *Arms and the Man*, and editor and writer of additional material for *A Variable Passion*. In 1973 he was assistant director of *The Marriage Brokers* at Stratford. A Stratford native, Mr. Hayes trained for three years at the Bristol Old Vic Theatre School in England. He was co-director of *The Caucasian Chalk Circle* and *A Midsummer Night's Dream* for the Verde Valley School in Arizona. Mr. Hayes has staged readings of original poetry, and his play *Summer and Fall* was workshopped at Stratford in 1981. In the 1983 Stratford season his play, *Blake*, was presented on The Third Stage, with Douglas Campbell in the *tour-de-force* role. His novel *American Slang* is currently under option to be filmed. Mr. Hayes is co-editor of the Stratford Festival Editions.

Michal Schonberg

Michal Schonberg is the Literary Manager of the Stratford Festival. His responsibilities include all the literary matters of the theatre, contacts with playwrights, scholars, and lecturers, as well as consultation on repertory. He is also co-editor of the Stratford Festival Editions. Associate Professor of Drama and Co-ordinator of Drama Studies at Scarborough College, University of Toronto. Mr. Schonberg has translated several works from Czech into English. He has also translated two of Tom Stoppard's plays, *Every Good Boy Deserves Favour* and *Professional Foul*, into Czech. He co-edited John Hirsch's adaptation of *The Dybbuk*, for publication and has had several works and adaptations published in *World Liberature Today* and *Modern Drama*. Mr. Schonberg prepared the 1982 Stratford version of *Mary Stuart* with translator Joe McClinton.

Stratford Festival Editions

available . . .

The Tempest
directed by John Hirsch

Macbeth
directed by Des McAnuff

As You Like It
directed by John Hirsch

The Taming of the Shrew
directed by Peter Dews

The Merry Wives of Windsor
directed by Robert Beard

A Midsummer Night's Dream
directed by John Hirsch

Romeo and Juliet
directed by Peter Dews and Steven Schipper

The Merchant of Venice
directed by Mark Lamos

For more information, write to:
Stratford Festival Editions
CBC Enterprises/Les Entreprises Radio-Canada
P.O. Box 500, Station A
Toronto, Ontario M5W 1E6